ONCE UPON A RHYME

IMAGINATION FOR A NEW GENERATION

2004 POET

Cheshire Vol II
Edited by Annabel Cook

 Young**Writers**

First published in Great Britain in 2004 by:
Young Writers
Remus House
Coltsfoot Drive
Peterborough
PE2 9JX
Telephone: 01733 890066
Website: www.youngwriters.co.uk

SB ISBN 1 84460 522 1

Foreword

Young Writers was established in 1991 and has been passionately devoted to the promotion of reading and writing in children and young adults ever since. The quest continues today. Young Writers remains as committed to engendering the fostering of burgeoning poetic and literary talent as ever.

This year's Young Writers competition has proven as vibrant and dynamic as ever and we are delighted to present a showcase of the best poetry from across the UK. Each poem has been carefully selected from a wealth of *Once Upon A Rhyme* entries before ultimately being published in this, our twelfth primary school poetry series.

Once again, we have been supremely impressed by the overall high quality of the entries we have received. The imagination, energy and creativity which has gone into each young writer's entry made choosing the best poems a challenging and often difficult but ultimately hugely rewarding task - the general high standard of the work submitted amply vindicating this opportunity to bring their poetry to a larger appreciative audience.

We sincerely hope you are pleased with our final selection and that you will enjoy *Once Upon A Rhyme Cheshire Vol II* for many years to come.

Contents

Charles Darwin Primary School

Jake Cummins (9)	14
Caitlin Thomas (9)	15
Bethany Tours (9)	15
Amanda Doyle (8)	15
Clare Hanson (9)	16
Heather White (9)	16
Mathew Griffiths (10)	17
Jessica Moore (9)	17
Belinda Howell (8)	18
Reece Christie (9)	18
Carrie-Anne Shaw (10)	19
Patrick McDonald (9)	19
Victoria O'Sullivan (10)	20
Rebecca Hunt (9)	20
Hannah Beasley (10)	21
Bethany Hayes (9)	21

Darnhall Primary School

Rachael Burrows (10)	22
Thomas Reddish (10)	22
Charles Johnson (10)	23
William Benjamin & Daniel Thomas (10)	23
Connor Matkin (10)	24
Jessica Clark (10)	25
Chloe Fleming-Scott (10)	26
Jason Halfpenny (10)	26
Emma Daniells & Nicole Walsh (11)	27
Caellan Murphy (9)	27
Danni Bersantie (7)	28
Chloe Robinson (8)	28
Callum Franchetti & Francis Davies (10)	29
Louis Elton (11)	29
David Banks (11)	30
Megan Harrison & Heidi Nagaitis (11)	31
Samuel Moreton (10)	32
Katie Knight (9)	33
Eric Sheriff (10)	33
Jessica Arnold (11)	34
Ryan Shaw (10)	34
Peter Long (10)	35

Rachel McDermott (9)	36
Jamie Norris (10)	36
Jessica McGurty (11)	37
Billie Shannon Mundy (10)	37
Alice Tainsh (10)	38
Daniel White (10)	39
Jennifer Ward & Charlotte Snelling (11)	40
Ashleigh Clewes (10)	41
Melissa Hayes (11)	42
Connor Eaton (10)	43

Eaton Primary School

Lucy Rogers (10)	43
Holly Himbury (9)	44
Alice Walsh (7)	44
Robyn Feast (10)	45
Andrew Bancroft (9)	45
Michael Bancroft (10)	46
Jordan Plimmer (8)	46
Emily Hill (11)	47
Katie Brownlee (7)	47
Lorna Douthwaite (10)	48
Catriona Baker (7)	48
Bethany Underwood (11)	49
Harriet Morris (7)	49
Ashley Louise Jones (10)	50
Michael Spencer (9)	50
Anna Rose Thompson (9)	50
Sarah Easby (9)	51
Alexander Wood (10)	51
Ryan Gaskell (7)	51
Oliver Fellows-Rosser (10)	52
Clare Chiddicks (9)	52
Bethany Gray (8)	53
Ryan Spann (9)	53
Sam Hooley (10)	54
Patrick Rourke (8)	54
Martin Craven (9)	55
William Latham (7)	55
Pria Mohindra (9)	55
Matthew Hill (9)	56

Charlotte Holt (9)   56
Daniel MacGillivray (8)   56
Jack Waters (7)   57
Lucy Oakeshott (9)   57
Ben Freeland (8)   57
Alexander Sinclair (7)   58

Flowery Field Primary School
Akash Khan (10)   58
Nathan Johnson (10)   58
Johura Alom (10)   59
Gillian Hesketh (10)   59
Jessica Davis (10)   59

Havannah School
Ciara Doran (9)   60
Chloe Stradling (9)   60
Jacob Bennett (9)   60
James Dodd (10)   60
Samantha Eastwood (9)   61

High Street CP School
Molly Carroll (8)   61
Cloe Norton (9)   61
Lilly Clulow (7)   62
Lucy Jane Foye (9)   62
Richard Cairns (9)   62
Catriona Stobie (8)   63
Sophie Pearson (8)   63
Eleanor Kittle (7)   63
Aimeé Elizabeth Eves (9)   64
Scott Bampton (8)   64
Devon Hughes (9)   64
Ella Davenport (8)   65
Michael James Butler (9)   65
Alex Baker (9)   65
Emily Louise Bullock (9)   66
Kyle Maddock (8)   66
Thomas Jonson Lamb (8)   66

Longbarn CP School

Ryan Roberts (9)	67
Molly Niklas (9)	67
Alice Wilshere (9)	68
Kiera Hampson (9)	68
Holly Jobes (9)	69
Christopher Birkett (8)	69
Gemma Elena Stubbs (9)	70
Sam Price (9)	70
Jessica Bebbington (9)	71
Ryan Retford (10)	71
Andrea Quigley (10)	72
Paige Maddock (10)	72

Lostock Gralam CE Primary School

Abigail Bircumshaw (6)	73
Jessie Jiao (6)	73
Daniel Hulse (9)	74
Shavaun Dutton (10)	74
Abigail Strickley (8)	75
Niall Fray (10)	75
Elliot Bailey (9)	76
Sasha Halsall (9)	76
Carly Insley (9)	77

Mansfield Primary School

Connor Preston (10)	77
Rachel Nield (11)	77
Lois Bowckett (9)	78
Danielle Williams (10)	78
Amy Riches (9)	78
Kristopher Jones (9)	79
Terri-Ann Hammond (8)	79
Kelly Rochell (11)	79
Izaac Allmark (8)	80
Hayley Davies (10)	80
Joshua Karl Jones (10)	80
Shaun Ridge (10)	81
Rebecca Weeks (9)	81
Jason Horgan (10)	81
Connor Lenton (8)	82

Zoe Wojtala Petterson (8)   82
Beccy Atherton (9)   83
Carly Bowckett (7)   83
Jordan Elwell   84
Lauren Peaurt (9)   84
Dean Bennett (9)   84
Curtis Ledsham (8)   85
Emma Rochell (7)   85
Charlotte Lenton (7)   85
Samantha Ogden (9)   86
Claire Atkins (8)   86
Jake Jones (7)   86
James Robert O'Regan (8)   87
Lucy Sweeney (8)   87
Daniel Longhorn (8)   87

Nether Alderley Primary School
Isabel Wilkinson (10)   88
Chloe Venables (10)   89
Edward Finch (10)   90
Ross Guirey (11)   91
Dylan Sumner (11)   92
Katherine Reynolds (10)   93

St Basil's Catholic Primary School, Widnes
Jemma Hawkes (10)   93
Rebecca Gill (10)   94
James Robertson (9)   94
Ryan Smith (9)   94
Abigail Irons (9)   95
Rebecca Dwyer (9)   95
Becky Taylor (9)   96
Kenny Sanderson (11)   96
Andrew Brookfield (10)   96
Chris Barton (11)   97
Hannah Conway (11)   97
Leanne Griffiths (11)   98
Lauren Maxwell (10)   98
Sam Brittles (9)   98
Liam Moores (9)   99
Kyle Ruane (10)   99

Elliott Hamlett (10)	99
Sam Argent (10)	100
Tom Hunter (10)	100
Adam Jackson (9)	101
Christopher Rose (10)	101
Matthew Naylor (9)	102
Daniel Saunders (9)	103
Ben Dourley (10)	103
William Hughes (9)	103
Josh McCann (9)	104
Daniel Hughes (10)	104
Martin Maguire (10)	105
Emma Moss (10)	105
James O'Donnell (10)	106
Simon Buckle (11)	106
Daniel Roberts (10)	107
Liam Ogburn (10)	107
Thomas Walsh (11)	108
Lewis Baines (10)	108
Alecia McWhirter (10)	109
Sean Franey (10)	109
Gemma Marshall (10)	110
Antony Marshall (9)	110
Hannah Fry (10)	111
Alexandra Rathbone (10)	111
Shaunie Lawton (10)	112
Hollie Chadwick (10)	112
Jake Larkin (9)	112
Jessica Roberts (11)	113
Daniel Newall (10)	113
Joshua Christopher (10)	113
Becky Sumner (10)	114
Hannah Oldfield (10)	115
Emily Pitt (10)	116
Adam Gee (11)	116
Tom Hague (11)	116
John Wise (10)	117
Jessica Washington (9)	117
Rebecca Gallagher (9)	118
Paige Geoghegan (10)	118

St Mary's Catholic Primary School, Crewe

Sabrina Moscati (9)	118
Hannah Spencer (10)	119
Natalie Matthews (9)	119
Vicki Perry (10)	119
Eleanor Simmons (10)	120
Martin Viashima (10)	120
Marc Waterhouse (9)	121
Lauren Penketh (10)	121
Elliott Oliver (9)	122
Alex Dopierala (9)	122
Rhiannon Graham (8)	122
James Hopley (10)	123
Joshua Mellor (9)	123
Ciaran Marks (9)	123
Siân Manfredi (9)	124
Jason Hodgson (9)	124
Samantha Patrick (9)	125

St Peter's RC Primary & Nursery School, Stalybridge

Lisa Wild (11)	125
Shannon Gilmore (11)	126
Joseph Lowe (7)	126
Daniela Agnello (11)	127
Louis Ridgway (7)	127
Adele Murphy (10)	128
Maxwell Burton (8)	128
Nathan Cox (10)	129
Jack Luby (10)	129
Lisa Sweeney (11)	130
Charlie Morton (11)	131
Tom Mulholland (11)	132
Ben Storey (11)	132
David Kempster (10)	133
Daniel Cox (8)	133
Cameron McDonald (7)	133
Antonio San José (10)	134
Antony Di-Fruscia (11)	135
Rebecca Simonaitis (10)	136
Bethany Austin (10)	136
Siobhan Fairclough (10)	137

Harry Moore (10)   137
Christopher Greenhalgh (10)   138
Amy Ashton (10)   138
Conor Trueman (11)   139
Kathleen Lister (10)   140
Hannah Welsh (8)   140
Georgia Curley (9)   141
Katie Bowers (8)   141
Annie Marshall (10)   142
Alex Danko (8)   142
Joseph Garside (10)   143
Heather Watson (8)   143
Holly Gummersall (10)   144
Siobhan-D'Arcie Holden (8)   144
Thomas Burgess (10)   145
James Garside (7)   145
Kerry Angus (10)   146
Bradley Lewis (7)   146
Kane Carty (10)   147
Robert Raymond (9)   147
Meagan Taylor (9)   148
Ryan Connor (9)   148

Shavington Primary School
Aimee Bates (10)   149
Ellie Hill (10)   150
Sam McKay (11)   150
Matthew Price (10)   151
Sophie Beeston (10)   151
Sam Bishop (11)   152
Daniel Gray (10)   152
Tom Edge (10)   152
Timothy Gallagher (10)   153
Rebekah Phillips (10)   154
Stephanie Verstraten (10)   154
Stephanie Sheer (10)   155

Sir John Offley CE (VC) Primary School
Jack Armstrong (8)   155
Ruby Nimbley (8)   155
Christopher Beech (10)   156

Whitby Heath Primary School

Laura Fletcher (8)	173
Melissa Williams (8)	173
Jessica Chambers (8)	173
Lori Bartley (11)	174
Harry Davies-Jenkins (7)	174
Helen Lyth (8)	175
Olivia Harvey (8)	175
Ashleigh Fletcher (10)	176
Tammie Binks (9)	176
Faye Barrett (8)	176
Hannah Weston (9)	177
Alisha Paige Heppell (9)	177
Zoë Ambrose (8)	177
Oliver Wedgwood (8)	178
Rebecca Donnelly (8)	178
Sophie Campbell (8)	179
Eve Pemberton (8)	179
Zoe Seymour (10)	180
Amy Hughes (9)	181
Chloë Moore (8)	181
Daniel Sheldon (8)	181

Wimboldsley Community Primary School

Samuel Clayton (10)	182
Charlotte Barber (9)	184

Woodfall Junior School

Helen Powell (10)	184
Jake Johnson (10)	184
Laura Pope (9)	185
Jemma Louise Anyon (9)	185
Megan Hall (9)	185
Wesley Osunjimi (8)	186
Catherine Halton (9)	186
Callum Reid (8)	186
David Nevin-Jones (8)	187
Rohan Littler (9)	187
Sophie Smith (9)	187
Jake Bayliff (8)	188
Georgina Peacock (9)	188
Leigh Maxwell (9)	188

Jack Hughes (7)   189
Ryan Green (9)   189
Ellie Jones (8)   189
Jack Mellor (8)   190
Esther Clarke (9)   190
Jessica Hall (9)   190
Joshua Cooke (7)   191
Chloe Metcalf-White (8)   191
Georgia-mai Timms (8)   191
Amy Jones (7)   192
Sean Lindley (8)   192
John Collins (9)   192
Rachel Knox (8)   193
Jacob Shepherd (8)   193
Alex Webb (9)   193
William Millington (7)   194
Jordan Stuart (7)   194
Sarah Maxwell (7)   195
Beth Lawley (8)   195

The Poems

Who Am I?

I am a . . .
Girl liker
Left-handed writer
Double dual
Fighter fuel
Nimber basher
Ball thrasher
Highway speeder
Big feeder
Disco diva
Dancing fever
Chocolate muncher
Bone cruncher
Liverpool fan
My name's Dan.

Dan Davenport (10)
Acresfield Primary School

I Am . . .

I am . . .
Gaming mad
Sometimes sad
Corrie lover
Unlike my brother
Hates maths
Likes baths
Wrestling liker
Sometimes biker
Oh gosh
My name's Josh.

Josh Willdigg (9)
Acresfield Primary School

I Am . . .

I am . . .

Earring bearer
Curly hairer

Animal lover
Fights with brother

Ghost story teller
Quite a good speller

Very loud screamer
And a daydreamer

Loves to be a dancer
Great prancer

Veggie hater
Homework later!

I'm an entertainer
And a bit insaner!

Rachel's my friend
Until the end!

I'm exoticly me
Watch out, you can see!

I love eating jelly
Guess what?
My name's Ellie!

Ellie Waite (10)
Acresfield Primary School

Lizzy (Elizabeth I)

There was a young lady called Lizzy
Who's hair was nothing but frizzy
She was so fast at sport
She was in the Royal Court
So they called her Frizzy Lizzy!

Jade Thornton (9)
Acresfield Primary School

Who Am I?

I am . . .
Nail biter
Story writer

Non-stop chatter
Big clatter

School later
Homework hater

Hot dog lover
Funny mother

Chocolate muncher
Sweetie cruncher

Nickname's Booze
Love to snooze

Special friends called Dan and Anna
Have you guessed?
My name's Susanna!

Susanna Rimmer (11)
Acresfield Primary School

Who Am I?

I'm a . . .
Glasses wearer
Child carer

Hard worker
Classroom lurker

Nail biter
Left-handed writer

Brill speller
Story teller

Number cruncher
Banana muncher

Have you guessed the game?
Mrs Sellers is my name!

Lily Smallman (11)
Acresfield Primary School

I Am . . .

I'm a . . .
Nail biter
Piano liker

Fussy eater
Sister beater

Running lover
Got no brother

Chocolate muncher
Crisp cruncher

Cheese hater
Homework later

I'm very chatty
But not fatty

Brown hairer
Book glarer

Have you guessed the game?
Emily is my name!

Emily Smith (9)
Acresfield Primary School

Kennings

School hater
Homework later

PE lover
Got no brother

Very clumsy
Got a mumsy

Brown hairer
Book glarer

Sweet muncher
Chocolate cruncher

Have you guessed the game?
Tali is my name.

Tali Jones (9)
Acresfield Primary School

Kennings

Messy roomer
Always groomer

Choccie muncher
Sweet cruncher

Lots of friends
To the ends

Scary movie taker
Noise maker

Accident prone
Always moan

Nice hair
Wear and tear

Always lazy
Mostly crazy

Sister kicker
Lolly licker

Daydreamer
Never meaner

I wanna have fame
Rachel's my name.

Rachel Coorey (11)
Acresfield Primary School

Bean Dan

There was a man called Dan
Who ate beans in a frying pan
He slurped his beans
And by all means
On beans there was a big ban.

Grace Marshall (9)
Acresfield Primary School

Haikus

Tigers

Pouncing predators
With their hard and padded feet
Tatooed with black stripes.

Summer

Burning sun beams down
Shines down on seaside swimmers
Tanned skin burns all day.

Camels

Kicking and spitting
Humps like very bad swollen backs
Walking really weird.

Matthew Thomas Stewart Pickett (11)
Acresfield Primary School

Kennings

Very small
Not tall
Quite chatty
Very ratty
Good running
Very stunning
Quite slim
Very dim
Bit crazy
Very lazy
Very titchy
My name is Richie.

Richie Hargreaves
Acresfield Primary School

Crusty

There was a clown called Crusty
He came from Maldusky,
Although he was a clown
His tricks were very rusty
And his house was very dusty.
Crusty had a girlfriend
Whose name was Ellladusker
Now Elladusker didn't like dust
She had a very bad allergy
She took one look at Crusty's home
And ran back to Maldusky.

Francesca Kokkinis (9)
Alderley Edge Community Primary School

Dogs

Here comes a scary dog,
He is as big as an eagle,
That big dog swims in bogs
And he eats a beagle.

A sausage dog comes on a lead
And they may look yummy,
They eat chips and beans
And they have a long tummy.

Marcus Finney (9)
Alderley Edge Community Primary School

The Gate

'The Gate', as it's called, the spooky old thing,
It sucks people in and turns them into the living dead,
But Ryan fought to the end . . . but he died, oh!
'The Gate' is the traveller's *death!*

Jason Edward Pollock (10)
Alderley Edge Community Primary School

A Cat

There was a cat,
That was very, very fat,
He walked down the road
And he was a big load.

He climbed a tree
And saw his friend Lee,
He jumped like a frog
And landed in a bog.

Splash, splash went the frog
In the very muddy *bog!*

Beth Toms (9)
Alderley Edge Community Primary School

Potty Parents

My dad is potty, my mum is spotty
My dad gets drunk, my mum is a punk
My mum is wild, my dad acts like a child
My mum acts like Cupid, my dad is stupid
And that's how parents are.

Helena Roberts (9)
Alderley Edge Community Primary School

The Cat

This is a cat that plays with a ball,
She puts it down and follows a mouse up a wall,
She grabs the mouse and throws it out of the door
And looks for more,
She finds one that she wants to catch,
The cat grabs the mouse and gives it a punch
And eats it for tea.

Esther Reid (9)
Alderley Edge Community Primary School

The Tiger

Here comes the tiger,
He is sharpening his claws,
Silently stalking,
He creeps with his paws.

The prey quietly grazes,
Gulping down the grass,
The tiger quietly gazes
And then at long last . . .

Up jumps the tiger,
Digging into the meat,
His enormous jaws grow wider,
The prey is killed
And the tiger has very achy feet.

The tiger kills a buffalo,
It starts to strip the meat,
It has a little snuffle,
At its very bloody feet.

Georgina Lucas (9)
Alderley Edge Community Primary School

The Wizard

There once was a wizard called Phil
Who tried to mix a spill
He went to the bath and sat on a raft
And boy, did he laugh.

Next came Will with a wand as big as a pill
Just as big as his friend Bill
He went to the sink to make his sword pink
But his wand turned out to be drink.

Last came Kill who wanted to fill his own wizard show
He popped right out and fought out to make a bowl of dough
He messed it up and popped a bell
And landed in a prison cell.

Luke James Foden (9)
Alderley Edge Community Primary School

Sweets

Haribos
Sherbets
Toffee bomb bombs
Pastels
Bubblegum gum
Yum, yum, yum!
Gobstoppers
Cream Eggs
De-li-cious!
Skittles
Laces
All in my tum!

Nicola Barney (9)
Alderley Edge Community Primary School

Limerick

There was a boy in the park
Who lay in the park and his name was Mark
He rolled down the hill and bashed into a mill
His dog barked and he made a mark
The cats lie as they got fed a pie
And the cats knew they did a poo.

Mark Petch (10)
Alderley Edge Community Primary School

Humphey

There once was a camel called Humphey
Who was very, very jumpy
He jumped all day
He jumped all night
And gave someone a big, big *fright!*

Ashleigh Nicholson (9)
Alderley Edge Community Primary School

Dogs

My dog is called Delilah
She jumps about
She runs about
I like to play football with her.

My dog is called Delilah
She sleeps a lot
She eats a lot
I like to tuck her in her basket.

My dog is called Delilah
She is black and white
She doesn't exercise at night
I like it when she rolls about.

Benjamin Tate Robinson (10)
Alderley Edge Community Primary School

Rhyming Couplets

My dog is small,
My cat is tall,
My mum is called Cheryl,
My gran is called Beryl,
My friend is called Esther Reid,
And is a good friend indeed,
My dad has brown hair
And people like to stare,
My cousin is thin,
As thin as a pin,
My cat caught a mouse,
It was running in the house,
I take my dog for a walk,
I always want to talk.

Emily Snape (9)
Alderley Edge Community Primary School

The Man

There was a man
Who hated pans.
He raced at Le Mans
And drank out of Coke cans.

He always won at Le Mans
'Cause his car had built-in fans.
Also built-in Coke cans,
But no built-in pans.

Graham Oxley (9)
Alderley Edge Community Primary School

My Dream

I went to bed last night,
My mum turned out the light,
I went to sleep,
By counting sheep,
Then I suddenly awoke,
In a thick crowd of folk,
Someone said, 'Follow me,
I'll take you to a door in a tree,'
So I went myself
And there saw an elf,
I went to take a closer look
And found that he was reading a book,
Then the elf spoke,
He said, 'Would you like a drink of Coke?'
'Yes,' I replied,
But then I accidentally knocked the curtain,
And found myself back in Burton,
In my room of pink and cream,
I realised it had all been a
Dream!

Sophie Wright (9)
Bishop Wilson CE Primary School

Green Cross Code

When you cross the road,
Use the Green Cross Code.

Look left, look right,
Make sure there's nothing in sight.

Look near, look far,
Look out for a car.

Listen there, listen here,
There just might be a car near.

Take one step on the road
And use the Green Cross Code.

Keep looking and listening,
'Cause a car might be whistling.

When you cross the road,
Use the Green Cross Code!

Yeah!

Jake Booth (11)
Bishop Wilson CE Primary School

The Past

First we have the Stone Age,
When lions roared when in a rage,
Then there is the Vikings,
Conquering was their liking,
Next come the Tudors with Henry,
Edward, Elizabeth and Mary,
There was the Georgians,
The vile of which they had their portions,
Then come the Victorians,
They were great historians,
Last we have our past,
Like the minute that's just gone so fast.

Caroline Turner (9)
Bishop Wilson CE Primary School

The Steam Train

On a dark, cold, wintry night,
Down to the station I went.
In came a grimy steam engine,
Fire blazing in the black,
Two green carriages pulling behind.
The gas lamps lit,
A comforting place on a cold winter's night.

The wind started blowing,
It started snowing,
Into the train I got.
It puffed away, far, far away
Before it stopped.

I got out,
To explore,
I found greenery,
On the floor.

I went back home,
Got into bed,
Fell asleep and in the morning said,
'I think I've been on a *ghost train.*'

Matthew James Collier (9)
Bishop Wilson CE Primary School

The House

Snow tumbles, turns like a white cricket ball being batted,
A large sheet of white blankets the Earth,
Frost performs itself over the snowy covered car,
Red car's tyres burn around trying not to be bombed by
                              white snowflakes,
Windows, a door even, covered in a frosty, white mixture,
                    like it has been cooked in a kitchen,
Hills, mountains being created out of this white mixture,
The house is a book of crafts.

Jake Cummins (9)
Charles Darwin Primary School

Distance

Screaming sun,
Sunset drifting over the sky forming a face of glee,
Gentle waves from the clear blue sea,
Children laughing,
Seagulls singing gracefully,
Pearl sea horses gliding,
A silent hand of rough wind,
Diamond reflection from the sun-glistened lilac sea,
Flowers shaped for the Queen, the England flag,
An ancient shopping centre built for thousands,
An elegant cross of icy water,
The mansion is a lively, beautiful, multicoloured fairground.

Caitlin Thomas (9)
Charles Darwin Primary School

Predator And Prey

Jaguar
Spotted killer
Running. Pouncing. Killing.
Fast. Orange. Black. Camouflaged.
Friendly. Gentle. Quiet.
Slow. Swimmer.
Tapir.

Bethany Tours (9)
Charles Darwin Primary School

Vampire Bat Haiku

Black-winged flying rat
Sucking blood from its live prey
Fluttering quickly.

Amanda Doyle (8)
Charles Darwin Primary School

The Minotaur

Once upon a moonlit sky,
Three peasants were doomed and then there was I,
It started with a ball of wool,
So I knew it was my job to fight the bull,
Slowly I pondered through the maze
And the lightning struck and made me gaze,
At the stars that shone so bright,
On this beautiful, wonderful, yet sinister night,
My eyelids grew heavy and I wondered why,
Why had they chosen me to suffer and die
And then I heard it, the Minotaur,
I heard his powerful, stomach quenching roar,
I took out my sword and with one big cry,
I knocked him over and made him *die!*

Clare Hanson (9)
Charles Darwin Primary School

The House

Yet again the autumn sunset glowed blood-red,
Mountainous piles of leaves scattered as a mighty wind blew,
Thick forest gathered around listening to an enchanting story,
                            but mountains found it dreadfully boring,
Upon these terrible mountains were gentle trickling streams,
Gusts of strong dragon breath made oak trees rustle,
Clustered around bases of strong oak trees, were mounds
                            of red brown leaves,
A breeze of wind was like a rush of icy frost,
Each rustle of a single tree was like a faint whisper of a deep,
                            deep secret,
The house was an enormous mound of rich earth.

Heather White (9)
Charles Darwin Primary School

Stephen Wiltshire's House

Around the luxurious house are shining, tall fences, sparkling,
Beyond the lovely house are glittering, emerald trees
Waving in the icy wind,
Beside, are pretty, gliding flowers
Fluttering peacefully,
Above are fluffy clouds flowing through a turquoise sky,
Beneath is a hard, square block of gold
Squeezed under the soft ground,
Inside is a lovely painted living room with brilliant ornaments,
Inside the room is a silver cage
Silently sitting in a lonely corner,
Inside the enormous cage
Was a slithery, poisonous python.

Mathew Griffiths (10)
Charles Darwin Primary School

The Rainforest

Sharp-beaked harpy eagle swoops through the tall trees.
Sly anaconda slides in-between branches into the muddy water.
Blue morpho butterfly flutters up and down.
Long-tailed spider monkey swinging from branch to branch,
                                                looking for fruit.
Giant armadillo snuffling across the leafy forest floor.
Scuttling bird-eating spider looking for prey.
Scarlet macaw floats across the sky, blue, red and yellow
                                                sparkling in the sun.
Winding lianas murdering the tall trees.
Tree porcupine, spikes in the air, climbs carefully.
Giant anteater digging in the soil, searching for tasty ants.

Jessica Moore (9)
Charles Darwin Primary School

The Rainforest

Venomous poison arrow frogs leaping from tree to tree.
Nectar-sipping bat gliding through the sky.
Howler monkey lonely and afraid.
Dark red blood of the spider monkey after the king jaguar
makes its mark.
Golden harpy eagle spying on its prey.
Shaking woodpecker hides in a hollow tree from dangerous
bird-eating spider.
Green quetzal zooming around without a care in the world.
Giant anaconda slithering down to the muddy water.
Mysterious chameleon changing colours ever so slowly.
Ruby-topaz hummingbird busy sucking up nectar.

Belinda Howell (8)
Charles Darwin Primary School

Rainforest

R uby-topaz hummingbird buzzing for nectar.
A giant anteater slurping up small brown ants.
I n the treetops animals live secretly, never known.
N umerous insects scuttle on the forest floor.
F rightening jaguars stalking prey.
O verhead the king vulture takes pride of place.
R are, beautiful butterflies seeking nectar.
E ating harping eagle ripping prey with a hooked beak.
S leeping three-toed sloth hanging from a branch.
T ree porcupine, spiky as thorns, rests quietly.

Reece Christie (9)
Charles Darwin Primary School

Stephen Wiltshire's House

Around the house is a pile of crackled leaves
Stiffened in the frosty wind,
Beyond the house is a fresh, clean canal,
Beside the house is a timbered farm
With a black and white cat
Sitting on a varnished fence,
Above the house are fragile clouds drifting,
Beneath the house is a colony of ants working in silence,
Inside the house is a large room with a table of glass,
Underneath this table is a box of gold belongings,
Inside the box and under the gold is a *spider!*

Carrie-Anne Shaw (10)
Charles Darwin Primary School

Rainforest

R are birds flying across the sky.
A rmoured armadillo eating quickly scurrying ants.
I ndian long-necked vulture focusing on its prey.
N ectar sipping bat looking for large flowers.
F ive baby toucans waiting for their mother to return.
O range-eyed jaguar seeking a meal.
R uby-topaz hummingbird busy sipping nectar.
E merald butterfly fluttering through the flowers.
S everal blue and yellow macaws flying in groups.
T ree porcupine eating juicy fruits.

Patrick McDonald (9)
Charles Darwin Primary School

The Cottage

A minute to midnight,
Snow falling like a dancer
Pirouetting in the coal-black sky,
Restless mountains tumbling
Into a panther-black sea.
Monstrous Welsh cows strolling
To the sea deserted beaches,
Kicking sand like candles,
Pitch-black caves,
Birds screeching,
Silently the cottage watches.

Victoria O'Sullivan (10)
Charles Darwin Primary School

Beach

Blazing summer's evening
As sunset twisted along the sky
Like an orange roller coaster,
A sandy, yellow beach with a disappearing horizon in the distance,
Waves swaying endlessly in the howling wind,
Sandy hills tornadoeing in the air,
Dull castle ruins surrounded by thick grey fog
And gigantic towering mountains,
Grey stone bricks of the remains tumble down
The emerald-green hill,
The house is a bed of flowers.

Rebecca Hunt (9)
Charles Darwin Primary School

Theseus

Theseus, mighty and strong,
Cheated on Princess Ariadne all along,
He defeated the Minotaur with the sword
And followed a ball of wool,
He left her on a Stranded Island
Where she did not know,
For this I shall go on,
For Theseus died a selfish man,
He deserved what he got,
As the day turns cold and grey,
These are the words I should say:
My heart is cold,
So selfish and blank,
I have a heart deep, deep down,
She still saw the selfish me
Still I betrayed her
And left her,
But I felt a little guilty
But so I said:
I felt weak and beginning to die,
So as I said with a sigh:
'I love you, Ariadne,
But I must still die.'

Hannah Beasley (10)
Charles Darwin Primary School

The Minotaur

He's mean, he's brave, he's a fighting arcade
With his horns and wicked eyes,
He's the most frightening giant inside.
You wouldn't want to meet him in the dark tide,
Beware in Crete for the labyrinth is near
And a creature quite well known,
The Minotaur.

Bethany Hayes (9)
Charles Darwin Primary School

The Lonely Shore

Out at the edge of the shore
A storm is brewing

Salty sand swirls in the icy wind
Thunder and lightning creeps round every corner,

Monstrous fog surrounds me
The dim light of a ship is lost as it comes into the harbour

The waves snatch the sand
Leading it to countries far,

Far,
Far,

The blizzard tries to snatch me
As I stand staring,

Staring,
Staring.

Rachael Burrows (10)
Darnhall Primary School

The Saint

All alone
No one around

I hear voices
Everywhere

People chanting
Death to all

Ring the bell
Open the door

And say
Go away!
Go away!
Go away!

Thomas Reddish (10)
Darnhall Primary School

In The Middle Of A Field

In the middle of a field
A man walks alone

The dark grass slashes at
His ankles with its millions of sharp fingers

And they freeze in the
Icy wind, they are still, still

He wanders, wanders:
He has no friends

In the middle of a field
A man walks alone
                alone
                alone!

Charles Johnson (10)
Darnhall Primary School

The Frozen Trees

Out at the edge of the river,
Where bony trees pinch,

Trees pinch the icy wind
And the river sways side to side,

Trees crack while they freeze,
In the icy air

And the breath of the trees
Try to communicate.

Trees shiver,
Under the shining moon,

Trees are alone,
Still and sturdy.

William Benjamin & Daniel Thomas (10)
Darnhall Primary School

The Cold Mountain

Out on the mountain peak
Where black clouds

Float around
In the night sky

And the sun
Fades away

And the thunder roars
Over the night sky

Wind follows it like a
Lonely traveller looking for a friend

A shadow appears in the
Moonlight

It is moving like a speeding cheetah
Hunting for food

He is a man searching
For a place to live

Heat is all he wants
He won't give up

He will fight to the bitter end

He sees a door and
Tries to get in

Knock!
Knock!
Knock!

Connor Matkin (10)
Darnhall Primary School

Child's Dream

Far away in a child's dream
Where golden horses run free

And where sugar plum fairies
Fly around all day

Where snow-capped mountains
Sway in the wind

And the sun sparkles
In the sky

Where painting take
Over the world

Where the clock ticks
Its last tick of time

And where little pink flowers
Twirl and dance in the wind

And where a knight wins
The first battle in the world

And where I
Become an angel

Where I fly around
On a magic carpet

But here in the heart of this
Little dreamworld
Somewhere is falling apart.

Jessica Clark (10)
Darnhall Primary School

The Seashore Beach

Out on the edge of the wavy sea
Where seaweed drowns,

As the waves begin to crack their tide
On a windy, early morning,

Where corals lay underneath the icy
Deep blue sea,

The breeze flows
Sweeping the sand away,

The sun is rising at the end
Of the sea, far, far away,

The eagles are flying
High above the sky,

Hear the eagles sing,
Hear the eagles sing,
Hear the eagles sing.

Chloe Fleming-Scott (10)
Darnhall Primary School

The End Of Time

Out on the edge of time,
Where colourless people

Stand still like silent statues,
In the black vacuum
And the trees
Stand tall like ghostly giants,
A lonely star is meandering
Through the clouds,
Slowly,
Slowly,
Slowly.

Jason Halfpenny (10)
Darnhall Primary School

Under The Sea

Right in the depths of the sea
Where no man has been before

Bubbles rise to the surface
Swelling the water above

Life surrounds the seabed
When a predator is coming

A fish wandering alone:

In
   And
Out
   And
In
   And
Out
Of the exotic coral

Not a care in the world
As it meanders through the Eastern Coast

Whales call from miles away
   Calling
      Calling
         Calling.

Emma Daniells & Nicole Walsh (11)
Darnhall Primary School

Snow

Snow came
And the sun was not lit up.
Nothing could move
In the coldness.
When the music began
One part of magic snow was revealed
To keep warmness safe.

Caellan Murphy (9)
Darnhall Primary School

Nana Lila

My nana was so caring to me,
I loved her blue eyeshadow and shiny, silver hair.
When she picked me up from school,
She had a warm cup of tea ready for me.

She always asked me,
'What have you done in school today?'
So I told her and she laughed with me.

Her house was always warm
And she always made me smile.
She made me feel safe and loved.

I loved her mashed potato
And smiley faces with beans.
She always had a Dairylea Dunker ready for me.

All these things made me feel loved
I'll always love you Nana, very much.

Danni Bersantie (7)
Darnhall Primary School

Candle

Candle flickering by the light,
Fire spreading
Each minute,
Dancing like a star,
Lighting your heart.
The light of the flame
Prickling,
Fire waving
On the
Slightest air.
Waves of
Red and
Orange
Flickering
In the darkness.

Chloe Robinson (8)
Darnhall Primary School

Beach Ball

In a
Corner
Of a beach

A flat beach ball
Lays in the sand
And a red crab is

Running around
Like a speeding
Cheetah on

A race
Track
Slowly

Stopping
And
Stopping.

Callum Franchetti & Francis Davies (10)
Darnhall Primary School

No Emotion

Lying there, in the middle of a cold, freezing field
Just there . . . effortless . . . no emotion,
The birds are killer hawks,
Waiting for the kill,
The boy turns over
And sits up,
His breath hangs in the air
Then the ice-cold wind snatches it away.
He walks in the field
And the millions of frozen fingers cut at his ankles,
He goes in the village
Knocks on a door and knocks
                    knocks
                    knocks.

Louis Elton (11)
Darnhall Primary School

The Frozen Man

Out on the edge of the forest
Where ghostly trees

Moan in the
Glittering moonlight

A figure
Cold and grey

Is walking
Stumbling . . .

Falling.

His cries of pain
Lonely and weak

Are swallowed up
By the wind.

The moon sniggers
The frost bites,

Yet the lonely man
Will not give up,

And with most of his strength,
He stands.

On and on
Into town

Strangers show
Him no mercy

A cold mist
Covers him

Making him glow
In the light,

He enters a
Garden, he

Knocks,
The door opens,
He faints.

David Banks (11)
Darnhall Primary School

The Stranger On The Mountain

On the highest hill,
On the highest peak,

Where Winter ruffles her coat of snow
And Spring never lingers long,
Someone is calling,

Calling,
Calling,

Someone is weak,
Someone is tired,

The wind whistles,
Hurriedly snatching the call for help,

In desperation the stranger fixes the blood-curdling wind
With an icy stare,

The clouds shiver when they hear the wind's roar,
Shaking like wet dogs,

The stranger's still calling,

Calling,
Calling.

Megan Harrison & Heidi Nagaitis (11)
Darnhall Primary School

Lonely

Out at the edge of town
Where the mud gurgles

Frantically wrestling with itself,
In this cold, dark, desolate place

Where the trees struggle for daylight
Trying to fight the army of fungus

And the atmosphere grows
Everlasting, evermore deadly

Paralysing everything in its path
Murdering every sign of life

A non-existing voice is
Echoing and echoing and echoing

Every explorer who had ventured there has never returned
Except one, who now has

Nothing but clothes
He has no family, no house, no love

So when he asks
For food

Give him some
Give him some
Give him some.

Samuel Moreton (10)
Darnhall Primary School

Before An Air Raid

Before an air raid . . .
I could see loads of people gathering up
I could hear a loud siren going off
I could feel people moving backwards and forwards
I could taste bits of tea in my mouth
I could smell egg on stoves.

During a raid . . .
I could see darkness all around
I could hear people coughing loudly
I could feel the hard floor where I was kneeling
I could taste all of the smoke
I could smell fire burning.

After the air raid . . .
I could see burnt down houses
I could hear children crying
I could feel heat from above
I could taste people coughing around me
I could smell fumes from all of the fires.

Katie Knight (9)
Darnhall Primary School

The Alphabet Of Horrible Habits

O is for Owen, who picks his nose.
P is for Peter, who wears girls' clothes.
Q is for Queenie, who never polishes her crown.
R is for Riley, who eats up the town.
S is for Sandy, who kisses frogs.
T is for Tina, who licks logs.
U is for Uncle James, who licks his toes.
V is for Vicky, who has a red nose.
W is for William, who kisses people's legs.
X is for Xavier, who covers himself in pegs.
Y is for Yasmin, who nicks plums.
Z is for Zena, who kicks people's bums.

Eric Sheriff (10)
Darnhall Primary School

The Church

Out on the edge of the church,
Where the Devil hangs around,

Just waiting till everybody has gone,
While the wind howls like an owl,

Making the bell sway side to side,
The graves are
Rotting
And
Rotting away

As the vicar locks up
The Devil is
Waiting
Waiting
Waiting.

Jessica Arnold (11)
Darnhall Primary School

Autumn Leaves

Leaves are yellow
Leaves are brown
Leaves are falling all around.

In my garden
On the ground
Falling lightly
Not a sound.

We can see in the playground
Piles of leaves
In a big mound.

When the leaves have all gone
That empty tree
Stands all alone.

Ryan Shaw (10)
Darnhall Primary School

The Midnight Woods

Out at the edge of a forest
Where skeleton trees

Grab out with their bony fingers
In the foggy mist

And bodies are swallowed
By the bottomless pit

And the rustles of bushes
As still as gravestones.

Hangs in the wind
Under the towering trees

A dark figure is moving
Around.

On the boggy, swampy ground
The figures shadowy

Feet
Creep
And
Creep

Here in a graveyard
In the heart of the forest

The crystals and statues are shining
Red and gold.

You can see the shining
Like you can see the sun

Breathe softly
Near a tree.

When the figure
Comes near the swamp

Run away,
Run away,
Run away.

Peter Long (10)
Darnhall Primary School

In The Air Raid

Before a raid . . .
I could see the commotion of people in the streets,
I could hear people's feet on the pavement,
I could feel cold air smothering my body,
I could taste nothing but the dryness of my mouth,
I could smell the damp, wet surface.

During a raid . . .
I could see people looking towards the ceiling,
I could hear bombs in the background,
I could feel the worries of people beside me,
I could taste the rubble from above,
I could smell the sweat and body heat.

After a raid . . .
I could see piles of brick where houses were,
I could hear the siren blasting out for the all clear,
I could feel my heart pounding inside of me,
I could taste the leftover acids,
I could smell the burning rubble.

Rachel McDermott (9)
Darnhall Primary School

The Alphabet Of Horrible Habits

O is for Owen, who picks his nose.
P is for Peter, who wears girls' clothes.
Q is for Queenie, who never polishes her crown.
R is for Riley, who eats the town.
S is for Sandy, who kisses frogs.
T is for Tina, who licks logs.
U is for Uri, who sleeps in the bin.
V is for Vicky, who always has to win.
W is for William, who lives outside.
X is for Xavier, who breaks the slide.
Y is for Yvonne, who eats mud.
Z is for Zelda, who runs around in the nud!

Jamie Norris (10)
Darnhall Primary School

Time

Out at the edge of time,
Where clocks tick,

They laugh as they move

Tick,
Tick,
Tick,

The tick stops
It's as still as night.

Clock alone,
Nobody else,

On a dark and misty road.

The clock
Ticks,
Ticks,
Ticks.

Jessica McGurty (11)
Darnhall Primary School

The Alphabet Of Horrible Habits

O is for Owen, who picks his nose.
P is for Peter, who wears girlie clothes.
Q is for Queenie, who never polishes her crown.
R is for Rita, who eats up the town.
S is for Sandy, who kisses frogs.
T is for Tina, who lives in a log.
U is for Ujeen, who smells like sweat.
V is for Victoria, who puts on bets.
W is for William, who eats grass.
X is for Xavier, who was cut by glass.
Y is for Yasmin, who always screams.
Z is for Zoe, who lives in streams.

Billie Shannon Mundy (10)
Darnhall Primary School

Cries

Out in the bleak atmosphere
Of the wide mountain range

There walks a man
A man so cold

That the wind
Racing past

Cannot feel him
Cannot feel him

And on the ground
Is a soft blanket of snow

And the air
Wanders confused with the wind

The man sits
And cries

He cries
He cries.

Alice Tainsh (10)
Darnhall Primary School

The Lost Child

In the heart of
The lost child
He is

Lonely,
Lonely,
Lonely.

He pictures his mum and dad far

Away,
Away,
Away.

He sleeps in the coldness, dreaming

Images,
Images,
Images.

At the edge of the child's heart
He is

Dying,
Dying,
Dying.

Daniel White (10)
Darnhall Primary School

The Edge Of The Ocean

Out at the edge of the ocean
By the roaring waves

I can see a ship
Going to stay with the sand

And the stern of the boat is bobbing
Up and down like a yo-yo

As it
Goes down

And down
And down

Fishes stare at the boat
As it ruins their homes

The fishes go looking for homes
They see big, black holes
　　　　　black holes
　　　　　black holes
　　　　　black holes
　　　　　black holes
　　　　　black holes.

Jennifer Ward & Charlotte Snelling (11)
Darnhall Primary School

Edge Of Eternity

Out at the edge of eternity
Where blanketed trees

Grab at the deserted space
Around them

And the emptiness freezes
On its shadow

And the frustrated, desperate call of the plants
Is silenced by the howling wind

A figure is standing
Alone:

On the icy roads
A figure is calling

Like a howling dog
In the darkness

The silence echoes
In the snow

Yet up on the edge of eternity
The blanketed trees are melting.

Ashleigh Clewes (10)
Darnhall Primary School

A Man Is Walking

Out at the edge of time
Where frostbitten trees scream in the icy wind

And the hedges dance
Through the night,

The breath of cattle
Freezes as the wind's fingers

Snatch it away
A man is walking alone:

On the dark road
His cold
Feet
Chime

And
Chime,

Here in a warm house
In the heart of time

A fire is burning bright
Red and yellow and gold,

You can hear the light
Like a wave

Lapping against the shore
In every room,

When the man who was walking
Comes to the door,

Open,
Open,
Open.

Melissa Hayes (11)
Darnhall Primary School

Graveyard

In the middle of a dark and misty graveyard
Where slimy gravestones loom in the darkness,

Where bony skeletons lurk in the moonlight
And werewolves feast on dead bodies,

Ghosts circle their graves to keep all trespassers away
While the fences grin at the graves

And all the graves say RIP engraved with blood!
And all is black while the sun rises,

All the bats are black as the dark
Atmosphere
Atmosphere
Atmosphere.

Connor Eaton (10)
Darnhall Primary School

Another Day In Paradise

Waiting for a lonely day
Thrown in a scrapyard sale
Nobody to be loved
I plead with all my hopes
My heart filled with anger
Every day I beg
Tears race down my cheeks
I bet with myself
I will get a home
Stood rock hard cold in the rain
People throw bottles at me
I'm so upset
I hate living here
I wait for an awful day
In a scrapyard
Once again.

Lucy Rogers (10)
Eaton Primary School

Another Day In Paradise

I am the most unhappy person.
And the most ignorable.
Each day I just lie there.
I sleep through the night, freezing.
Help me get to paradise.
Never seen anyone else on the streets.
Apart from me.
I seem to be the only one.
Everyone else is lucky.
Is it only me?
Help me get to paradise.
Begging to people on the streets.
Crying every night.
I miss my family.
I hope I get adopted by friendly people.
It's nearly Christmas.
One present please.

Holly Himbury (9)
Eaton Primary School

The Scrapyard

It was a fiery day
Sun shining on rusty cars.
Metal bars tilted like the Titanic as my reflection faded into rust.
Rats scurrying under cars, slipping off cranes.
I smelt burnt food from the mountain of cookers.
I took a look in an old car.
Mice were getting comfy, snuggling up.
My eye caught a digger, dripping,
Silently crying and drooping on the ground.
It was turning into evening.
The metal looked like it blinked.

Alice Walsh (7)
Eaton Primary School

Why Did I Leave Home?

I say to people on the streets
Please give me a home.
But all they do is jog past
As if I'm not there.
London streets aren't a place
You would want to live in.
It's dark and sooty and nobody cares
About you.

Why did I run away from my loving family
That loves me?

When I pass the shops all I can see
Is a dirty, lost and lonely girl
That wishes she had some supper.

Why did I run away from my loving family
That loves me?

If you are reading this, don't do what I did
Running away from home isn't something
That you would want to do.

Robyn Feast (10)
Eaton Primary School

One For The Rumble Of The Awaking Volcano

One for the rumble of the awaking volcano,
Two for the footsteps of the sly jaguar,
Three for the launch of the exploding rocket,
Four for the horn of the titanic rhino,
Five for the call of the proud cockerel,
Six for the flames of the long-lost dragon,
Seven for the shield of the heroic knight,
Eight for the bow of the divine archer,
Nine for the poison of the fanged viper,
Ten for the craters of the twilight moon.

Andrew Bancroft (9)
Eaton Primary School

Another Day In Paradise

I am a very pale and slim boy.
People like me live on the streets,
Trying to snatch out a living.
It feels like my hopes have gone.
It started when my mother and father
Lay me outside.
I can't get that thought out of my head.
I'm slowly, but sadly
Walking to my mat
Where I have little naps every day.
I'm desperate all the time,
I smell like the drain,
I don't know how people like me
Cope with lives like mine.
This is terrible.

Only one day on the streets,
Found a job and I don't get much
I scrub these people's kitchen and floors
For payments.
I feel sometimes to nick valuable things
When families are not around.

People laugh at me and pull faces.
This life stinks
I want to die,
Oh, someone help me.

Michael Bancroft (10)
Eaton Primary School

Eel

Eel soft as baby's cheeks,
Swims through salty sea.
Sea rises up.
Slimy eel riding the water,
Playful as a puppy.

Jordan Plimmer (8)
Eaton Primary School

Another Day In Paradise

Six years of being homeless -
Been thrown out.
Empty-hearted,
No one loves me.
Hopes and dreams,
Someone will come for me.

Ragged dress,
Dirty face,
Greasy hair.

Only a small blanket,
Nobody to trust,
So helpless,
Afraid,
Frightened,
I will die here!
Please somebody help!

Emily Hill (11)
Eaton Primary School

The Lion

The lion is the king of the beasts
His walk is full of grace
His fur superb in moonlight
Mane light as the sun of day
Huge paws like drums
Tail swishes from side to side
Eyes amber as traffic lights
Very strong
His run is like a leap
Brave lion
The biggest cat.

Katie Brownlee (7)
Eaton Primary School

Another Day In Paradise

The man who used to be my dad,
He doesn't care whether I live or die,
We had an argument that turned sour.
But how did it end like this?

Sleeping in the rubbish,
My face turns cold with rage.
Why should I live in despair?
How did it end like this?

No possessions to call my own
And every penny worth more than ever,
People just walk past.
Why should I live a life?
How did it end like this?

Through all the days of loneliness
And all the nights of sorrow,
Only one question rings in my mind . . .

How did it end like this?
No clothes, food or shelter.
How did it end like this?
No friends or family to love me.
How did it end like this?
No future to look forward.
How, oh how, did it come to this?

Lorna Douthwaite (10)
Eaton Primary School

The Snow

Snow was falling like a punch in the chest.
My cheeks felt as cold as ice cubes.
Delicate snowdrops fell onto my cold, stiff hair.
Water trickled down my freezing arms and legs.
Snowflakes pranced and danced finding their friends.

Catriona Baker (7)
Eaton Primary School

Another Day In Paradise

Sleeping between two shops,
Hunched with one small blanket,
Crying for help.

Freezing by night,
Soulless by day,
Crying, crying for help.

Day after day, begging,
No mercy or pity is returned,
A stranger passes
He takes one glance,
My hopes are high but plummet once again,
Pleading for help.

I should blame myself,
Regretting the day I ran.
Thought it was cool,
Found out it was not.
Pleading, pleading for help.

Grease in my hair,
Rags for my clothes,
A home
Food
Clothes,
But that's a dream.
Being loved.
Held by a family,
But as I said a dream.

Bethany Underwood (11)
Eaton Primary School

My Amulet

Inside the silver stone there is a time when we were together.
My mum's locket when she was a little girl.
A little Spanish shell which I found when I went to Spain.
Inside my heart bracelet I see my whole family.

Harriet Morris (7)
Eaton Primary School

My Mummy

My mummy is magical,
She reminds me of my rabbit,
She is a silver birch,
Her skin is like soft fur,
Her eyes are as brown as velvet,
Her voice is as powerful as a lion,
She says, 'You are a sweetheart, Ashalou,'
I feel she is a golden angel.

Ashley Louise Jones (10)
Eaton Primary School

My Mum

My mum is enchanting.
She reminds me of a princess.
She is a beautiful apple tree blossoming.
Her skin is like a beauty specialists.
Her eyes are as green as a sweet, juicy apple.
Her voice is as smooth as silk.
She says, 'You're lovely' to me.
I feel as though I'm the luckiest kid in the world.

Michael Spencer (9)
Eaton Primary School

Aslan

Mane, a seashore of sand.
Rainbow eyes full of laughter and love.
Softly his paws go over the crumbly sand.
Aslan is powerful and caring.
Trustworthy and unbeatable.
Fur round his gorgeous face.
With his magical eyes he makes himself happy.

Anna Rose Thompson (9)
Eaton Primary School

My Great Grandma

My grandma is as elegant as a butterfly.
She sits on her armchair all day long.
She is always giving me money.
She has teeth that aren't real,
Hair white as snow,
Wears glasses,
Babysits for dogs,
Kind to everyone.
My grandma is as sweet as a lollipop.

Sarah Easby (9)
Eaton Primary School

Aslan Poem

His mane is like the glorious sun.
Heart full of honesty and wisdom.
Legs as big as you and me.
Never looks angry, but sometimes sad.
Wonderful motionless head.
Paws crash to the floor and make it crumble.
Heart of gold.
Fabulous wavy fur.
He has untouchable love.

Alexander Wood (10)
Eaton Primary School

Sunflower

Sunflower petals sparkle like the sun in the sky.
Dark centre, the darkest shade of brown;
Round like the sun.
Stem tall, green and thick, like a tree trunk;
Sunflower seeds lovely to eat.

Ryan Gaskell (7)
Eaton Primary School

My Life

Imagine living on the streets
In a rain-soaked cardboard box.
Sad, sunken eyes hiding secrets from a past life,
Hating the new one.

Embarrassed humiliation,
Afraid to show my face to the world.
Feeling like an empty soul,
With no hope in sight.

People push me aside with a disgusted look,
Or toss a coin in my old, ragged hat.
Not a care in their seemingly happy lives,
As they pass me by.

So, ask yourself how would you feel?
Hopes and dreams for the future destroyed,
With no one to trust,
This is my life.

Oliver Fellows-Rosser (10)
Eaton Primary School

Eel

Sea strong like a rock,
Eel follows its senses,
Eel slimy as a snake,
Water colder than ice,
Slithering bodies swim round,
Blackcurrant bulging eyes watch,
Sargasso Sea my favourite place,
Elver body looks like glass,
Weeds wave silently,
Seagulls swoop from the sky,
Eel slides like a snake,
Crystal willow leaves swim.

Clare Chiddicks (9)
Eaton Primary School

A Midsummer Night's Dream

Magical fairies dancing while hovering in the sky,
Disappearing and appearing;
Amazing and dazzling,
Wings beating together in the air.
Little shining lights floating silently in different colours.
Playful creatures singing and dancing in the moonlight,
Like little stars.
All rare and enchanting.
Little shy people, wise and graceful glowing dots.
Big glistening wings fluttering on fairies' backs.
Shining little creatures.
Strange fairy emerges from the dark forest.
Slanted small eyes glowing in the dark
Branches hanging from big eyebrows.
Twigs and leaves in a long beard.
Glittering silver hat
Long hair streaming below it.
Little people circling round the moon.

Bethany Gray (8)
Eaton Primary School

My Grandad

My grandad is as popular as a celebrity.
He likes making people laugh.
He likes having toast and a few cups of tea.
His glasses sparkle like the sea.
He laughs like a hyena.
His hair is as spiky as a hedgehog.
His hands are as bumpy as a reindeer's antlers.
He knows how to help.
He's straight as the road.
But best of all,
He's mine!

Ryan Spann (9)
Eaton Primary School

Another Day In Paradise

I drift like a dead leaf along the road.
Just over an argument.
I was quickly dragged out of my home.
I wander the streets with a broken heart.
'Will anyone take me home?'
I call out, but only silence replies back to me.
People walk through me and smash my heart.
Men and women look at me disgustedly.
Shouting at me to get out of their way.
I feel I am trapped in darkness.
Why don't I just die?
I bellow out but no one answers me.
I say to myself 'I exist.'
Everyone else says I don't.
Every time I awaken.
It's another day in paradise for others.

Sam Hooley (10)
Eaton Primary School

Aslan

Great lion
Mane a blizzard gathering around his head
Eyes like a white flame
Paws soft as a white fox.
Claws as sharp as a knife
Head like a giant fire
Teeth sharp as a sabre-toothed tiger
Legs strong as a brick wall
Fierce as you have ever seen
Tail as fast as the wind
Roar as loud as thunder
Fur as golden as the sun.

Patrick Rourke (8)
Eaton Primary School

My Mother

My mum is kind and generous.
She reminds me of the colour green.
She is a beautiful silver birch tree.
Her skin is like a soft rabbit.
Her eyes are as good as Rice Krispies.
Her voice is like the lovely wind.
She says to me, 'Go to bed now.'
I love her so much that she is a star.

Martin Craven (9)
Eaton Primary School

Eel

The sea is deep
The waves are strong
Seaweed is slimy
It wraps around the eel
Waves crash on the rocks.

William Latham (7)
Eaton Primary School

Eel

The sea is dark and as deep as a forest.
Eel slimy to touch,
Eats with his fierce jutting mouth.
Teeth like a very sharp saw blade.
Eyes like big bulging blackcurrants.
Born like a willow leaf.

Pria Mohindra (9)
Eaton Primary School

Aslan Poem

Aslan is dazzling and unbeatable
Caring and powerful with knowledge and strength.
Eyes like a golden jewel
Dashing, beautiful, lovely paws.
His voice is quietly spoken.
Respectful and kind
His soft head shiny and great
Caring and gentle
Teeth big, sharp and shiny.

Matthew Hill (9)
Eaton Primary School

Aslan

Aslan is kind and loving.
When you look at him you see glimpses of dazzling eyes.
Aslan is bright and royal, but also terrifying,
Mane like fire,
Eyes as flame, full of magic,
Wonderful paws slicing through the grass.
Seriously sharp claws, like razors.

Charlotte Holt (9)
Eaton Primary School

Amulet

Inside the dog's claw, a stony wall;
Inside the stony wall, the dog's fur;
Inside the dog's fur, the muddy canal;
Inside the muddy canal, the dog's eyes;
Inside the dog's eyes, the glistening sun;
Inside the glistening sun, the dog's claw.

Daniel MacGillivray (8)
Eaton Primary School

A Footballer's Amulet

Inside a gold ring, is Mum and Dad's wedding.
Inside my dog's fur, are the snow and ice.
Inside my dad's hair, are the stone and the sand.
Inside my teddy, are safe things.
Inside the pebble, are the sea and the shell.
Inside my football keyring, are crystal and metal.
Inside crystal and metal is a game of football.

Jack Waters (7)
Eaton Primary School

Aslan

Mane like a golden fur ball.
Royal teacup eyes.
Sandy paws collide across crumbly floor.
Stern back moves gently across the ground.
Great head looking for danger.
Loving and caring to everybody
Never getting scared.

Lucy Oakeshott (9)
Eaton Primary School

Amulet

For Digger, my puppy dog, a bit of his black hair;
For Toffee, my other dog, a sheep's white bone;
For the beach, a smooth pebble;
For an old car, a bit of its rough tyre;
For my dad, his penknife;
For my mum, a piece of her beautiful, soft hair.

Ben Freeland (8)
Eaton Primary School

In My Amulet

I look at Robby dog's picture,
I see him playing on the golf course.
I hug Blue Ted and I feel calm.
I touch my blanket and I have happy feelings.

Alexander Sinclair (7)
Eaton Primary School

Cinquain

Spooky
Cool blood chilling
Something shivers my spine
Terrified anticipation
Screaming!

Akash Khan (10)
Flowery Field Primary School

Winter's Charms

A thin sheet of crystalline frost lies upon the ground,
I walk into a mist,
My feet crunch on the snow,
My breath curls before me like cold fire.
I see the spells of winter,
I feel the chill coating me,
I hear nature's melodies being played.
The icy wind armours me from warmth,
The fog's like a whip of Arctic ice,
I return home to the warm fire,
The spirits of winter call,
I feel replenished by the flames.

Nathan Johnson (10)
Flowery Field Primary School

Winter And Me

On a cold, snowy winter's day,
I went out in the frost to play.
My friend and I had a snowball fight,
We played under the silvery moonlight!
Built a snowman halfway through,
We even built an igloo!
Feathery snowflakes in the sky,
Drifting up so high, high, high.
I love winter!

Johura Alom (10)
Flowery Field Primary School

Wintertime

Frosty
Numb fingers tingle
Biting wind nibbles my face
Shivers, freezing on my body
Icy.

Gillian Hesketh (10)
Flowery Field Primary School

Springtime Cinquain

Springtime
White fluffy lambs
Pretty blossom on trees
Wonderful, new things all around,
So sweet.

Jessica Davis (10)
Flowery Field Primary School

Limerick

There once was a man from Stoke
Who thought everything was a joke
He went to the shop
For a bottle of pop
But cried when he found he was broke.

Ciara Doran (9)
Havannah School

White

White is a rushing tear down a sad face.
It's a long, milky stream.
White is a baby swan calling all alone,
It's a broken heart with no soul,
It's a lonely cloud left in the sky.

Chloe Stradling (9)
Havannah School

What Am I?

I look like a small, podgy boy,
I eat greedily from a trough,
I move slowly on four stumpy legs,
I love to roll around in the mud,
I live on a farm but don't lay eggs.

Jacob Bennett (9)
Havannah School

What Am I?

I look slithery and slimy
I move fast, sometimes slow
I love to eat meat
But I don't like the snow.

James Dodd (10)
Havannah School

Black Is . . .

A solid voice towering over me
A lonely town at midnight
It sounds like a screaming death
In a graveyard
It's losing someone you love
A heart ripped into a million pieces
It's a dirty trick when you're innocent
It sounds like hatred
It is the moonlit sky
Black is thunder and lightning.

Samantha Eastwood (9)
Havannah School

The Pool

Crystal clear, clear as crystal,
Glimmering, gleaming, shimmering, shining.
When I look into my pool,
I see the beautiful things of the Earth.
Butterflies, flowers, sun and moon,
Grass and birds in trees
And young romantic scenes.

Molly Carroll (8)
High Street CP School

Autumn

Autumn leaves all different colours,
Yellow, brown and orange.
Whisper softly because the birds are hibernating in the trees.
The trees are rotten with no leaves on.
It has only got its arms on with no hands.
Swishing side to side making a lovely sound.

Cloe Norton (9)
High Street CP School

Trees In Winter

T rees, trees, so snowy white
R elax all day, the trees are there
E very day
E ven when it's
S nowing heavy, trees are beautiful.

I n wintertime it's so beautiful
N ever cry, go outside and see the trees.

W inter's great!
I t's wonderful
N ever fear, the trees are here
T ry it out, winter's here.
E verybody's having fun, with trees
R elax all day, because it's fun! Trees, trees!

Lilly Clulow (7)
High Street CP School

Class Eight

C ome to Class Eight
L ively with love and care
A musing and funny
S miley like the sunshine
S uch an energetic class. That's us.

Lucy Jane Foye (9)
High Street CP School

Elephant

The tremendous elephant
Is as fast as can be
Gives no chances
Eager for food
Rampaging through Africa.

Richard Cairns (9)
High Street CP School

Liverpool

L ucky Liverpool win 1-0.
I love Liverpool, they're the best, they're
V ery good, but if only they were top of the league.
E veryone loves Liverpool everyone except Harry
R eally loves Man U, they
P ut their boot in.
'O w,' Owen cries as he hits the ground.
O h no! He's injured!
L iverpool rock!

Catriona Stobie (8)
High Street CP School

The Playground Haikus

The playground is still
Then children come out to play
They all play, happy.

Together we play
And have lots of fun, hooray
Then we all go home.

Sophie Pearson (8)
High Street CP School

The Dragon

D ragons are dreadful
R aging rounds of fire he blows
A bsolutely unstoppable
G iants are terrified
O f the ferocious dragon
N o one dare fight it.

Eleanor Kittle (7)
High Street CP School

Elephant

E normously huge
L azy and fat
E legant skin
P lunging through the jungle
H uge and mighty
A cting huge
N aughty and greedy
T all and fat.

Aimeé Elizabeth Eves (9)
High Street CP School

Football

F eet are crucial to play,
O ut, in, out, in,
O ut, in, out, in,
T op corner, Owen,
B all control boy,
A ll the time, ball control
L ong ball, long ball,
L eave it now, we've scored a goal.

Scott Bampton (8)
High Street CP School

Dungeon

D ark, gloomy and horrible
U nderground the floor there is a dungeon
N ot a nice place to live
G ungy and disgusting
E very night it's smelly
O n the floor, bones and bodies
N ever back in the dungeon. Freedom, complete freedom.

Devon Hughes (9)
High Street CP School

Tiger

Huge
Mighty
Energetic
Tiger
With a swipe of a paw
An elegant swipe
A powerful swipe
A wonderful creature
It would be terrible for you to leave this world.
Tiger
Oh, elegant tiger.

Ella Davenport (8)
High Street CP School

Dungeon

D ark and gloomy, scary and freaky.
U nderground where rats crawl and skeletons hang like ghosts.
N ot nice when you get chained up.
G hosts are everywhere and they frighten you.
E nd of the dungeon the light is up the ladder.
O ne day the boy got out of the dungeon.
'N ight,' said Mum and he had a great dream.

Michael James Butler (9)
High Street CP School

Dungeon

D ark, pitch-black, as dark as space.
U nderground, never try to go in.
N aughty people get thrown in.
G ungy and dark with guard dogs.
E very day people get caught snooping around.
O n the floor cannon balls get thrown.
N ever go in the dungeon because you won't come out.

Alex Baker (9)
High Street CP School

Dog

Cuddly
Cute
Furry
Dog
They love walks with you
Smelly
Sometimes dangerous
If we didn't have them
The world would be unhappy
Dog
Oh, you lovely dog.

Emily Louise Bullock (9)
High Street CP School

Dungeon

D ark and gloomy, quiet too.
U nderground floor, mouldy and wet.
N ot a very nice place to go.
G unge on the walls, smelly as well.
E very night it's pitch-black.
O n the wall, blood and bones.
N ever go to the dungeon.

Kyle Maddock (8)
High Street CP School

Santa

S anta comes once a year
A nd he brings presents
N ot for revolting and naughty children
T hen he has an enormous rest
A nd comes back next year.

Thomas Jonson Lamb (8)
High Street CP School

Space

I can see shooting stars sparkling with light,
I can touch the control panel with so many buttons,
I can hear the countdown of mission control,
I can hear the booming of the engine,
I can touch the weightless drink,
Will we make it to the moon?
Neil Armstrong's footprint on the moon forever,
Everything still and quiet,
Questions and breathing,
Asteroids zooming past,
On the moon the Earth looks like a marble,
Inside the rocket zooming,
American flag,
The roaring engine,
Will we make it back?

Ryan Roberts (9)
Longbarn CP School

Lion

As it stumbles,
Across the cage to and fro,
He thinks about other things,
He could be doing,
Like running and playing,
But all he has is a cage.

As the owner of this poor creature,
Throws him one piece of meat,
He thinks about what he could be doing,
Like running free and catching his own food,
But someone has to do it for him.

Think of how lucky other animals are,
Then think of him.

Molly Niklas (9)
Longbarn CP School

I Need You!

I need you!

Like a coat needs a zip
Like an apple needs a pip
Like a finger needs a tip

I need you!

Like a start needs an end
Like a corner needs a bend

I need you!

Like a kid needs a mum
Like a tree needs a plum
Like a hand needs a thumb

I need you!

Like a body needs a soul
Like a train needs coal

I need you!

Alice Wilshere (9)
Longbarn CP School

My Family Is Weird, But Not Me!

My Juce is bad, my mum is mad
My sister is a pain and my brother's called Wain
My family is weird, but not me,
But when my mum goes to the shop
She always brings her mop, mop, mop
But when I go to the shop
I always buy some pop, pop, pop
My family is weird, but not me
Why, why, why is it me!

Kiera Hampson (9)
Longbarn CP School

I Need You!

I need you!

Like a plant needs water
Like a brick needs mortar
Like a mother needs a daughter

I need you!

Like a bunny needs legs
Like a chicken needs eggs
Like washing needs pegs

I need you!

Like a button needs a hole
Like a man needs a pole
Like a footballer needs a goal

I need you!

Holly Jobes (9)
Longbarn CP School

I Need You!

I need you!

Like a bank needs money
Like a bear needs honey
Like a bee is funny

I need you!

Like a sky needs a sun
Like a cheetah needs some fun
Like a baker needs a bun

I need you!

Like a dog needs a walk
Like a bird needs a squawk
Like my friends need to talk.

Christopher Birkett (8)
Longbarn CP School

I Need You!

I need you!

Like a bunny needs its legs
Like a chicken needs its eggs

I need you!

Like a model needs a pose
Like a garden needs a rose

I need you!

Like a school needs a teacher
Like the world needs a creature

I need you!

Like a cat needs its bed
Like a child needs its ted

I need you!

Gemma Elena Stubbs (9)
Longbarn CP School

Selkie

I saw a selkie sitting by the sea,
Sad and happy eyes all in a flash.
Jumping in and out of the water.
Sparkling in the shining air.
Water crashing against the rocks.
A beautiful face looking puzzled.
Combing her hair in the sunlight.
Gone forever.

Sam Price (9)
Longbarn CP School

I Need You!

I need you

Like a leopard needs its spots
Like the flowers need the pots

I need you

Like a foot needs a shoe
Like the ocean needs the blue

I need you

Like the drainage needs the pipes
Like the tiger needs the stripes

I need you

Like a ball needs a kick
Like a bomb needs a tick.

Jessica Bebbington (9)
Longbarn CP School

I Need You

I need you . . .
Like a sun needs a sky
Like a spider needs a fly
Like a baker needs a pie

I need you . . .
Like a bank needs money
Like a bee needs honey
Like Easter needs a bunny

I need you.

Ryan Retford (10)
Longbarn CP School

I Need You!

Like a tiger needs its stripes
Like a toilet needs its pipes

I need you!

Like a cat needs a tail
Like slime needs a snail

I need you!

Like the sea needs a fish
Like a spoon needs a dish

I need you!

Like a race needs an end
Like I need a friend

I need you!

Like Christmas needs a turkey
Like space needs Mercury.

Andrea Quigley (10)
Longbarn CP School

You!

You! Your hair is like cola laces!
You! Your eyes are like pickled onions!
You! Your lips are like ripe red cherries!
You! Your ears are like Play Doh shapes!
You! Your ring is like tinfoil!
You! Your body is like a hot dog!

Paige Maddock (10)
Longbarn CP School

Look

Look at the raindrops
Dripping, dropping
Through the trees.

Look at the foxes
Big bushy tails
Rushing through the trees.

Look at the badgers
Black and white faces
Coming out in the midnight sky.

Look at the squirrels
Lovely, soft grey fur
Running up the trees.

Look at the rabbits
Silky soft fur
Hopping around the forest.

Abigail Bircumshaw (6)
Lostock Gralam CE Primary School

Look

Look at the raindrops
Dripping, dropping
Through the trees.

Look at the black lake
Deep and black
Muddy water.

Look at the rabbit
Hopping and jumping
Through the forest.

Jessie Jiao (6)
Lostock Gralam CE Primary School

Sharks!

Sharks! Sharks!
Swim all day,
When they want to play,
They swim around
Seeking prey.

Eating anything in their way.
Great thick skin,
What is their fear?
Their one thousand teeth.

Sharks! Sharks!
Swim all day
When they want to play,
They swim around
Seeking prey.

Daniel Hulse (9)
Lostock Gralam CE Primary School

Snow Tiger

Tiger! Tiger! Cubs at night
Find them sleeping very tight
Close by you by the light.

Hungry for food
Make sure you're not in a mood
Your mum has just caught meat
All squabbling to be fed.

Claws as sharp as a razor
With eyes like a laser
Pointy ears with white body
Tail lashing the ground
Created by God
Running through snow.

Shavaun Dutton (10)
Lostock Gralam CE Primary School

Horses

Horses! Horses! Every day going to play in the hay
Galloping here! Galloping there! Galloping!

Horses are fit to play
And trot around and walk and neigh.

Horses! Horses! Every day going to play in the hay
Galloping here! Galloping there! Galloping!

Horses eat and eat
And eat hay and grass, one of each.

Horses! Horses! Every day going to play in the hay
Galloping here! Galloping there! Galloping!

Horses! Horses! In their stable pregnant with foals
The mother horse is tired and weak with a foal.

Horses! Horses! Every day going to play in the hay
Galloping here! Galloping there! Galloping!

Abigail Strickley (8)
Lostock Gralam CE Primary School

Dragon! Dragon!

Dragon! Dragon! Flaming bright
In the land of night
Scales like diamonds, hard as rock.

Monster devil, killing life
World its home, killer might.

Dragon! Dragon! Flaming bright
In the land of night
Scales like diamonds, hard as rock.

Niall Fray (10)
Lostock Gralam CE Primary School

Kangaroos!

Kangaroos! Kangaroos!
Play all day
What strange food do you eat?
Is it bushes? Is it leaves?
Why is your pouch so big?

What is your fear?
Do you hop all day?
Do you sleep for the night?
Do you play with your joey?

Kangaroos! Kangaroos!
Play all day
What strange food do you eat?
Is it bushes? Is it leaves?
Why is your pouch so big?

Elliot Bailey (9)
Lostock Gralam CE Primary School

Dogs

Dog, you are so loud barking, scratching, squeaking.
Lying on the couch squirming, wriggling, pouncing.
Go run away, leave me in peace,
So far you'll go, then get tired.

Are you gonna come back?
Raw meat is here for you,
Come and eat it and wolf it down.

Come on, I'm waiting for you,
Come back soon,
With your barking and squirming,
I miss you dog, please come back.

Sasha Halsall (9)
Lostock Gralam CE Primary School

Kittens, Kittens, Kittens!

K ittens, kittens come for your food
I n the darkness of the night
T rot, trot to your basket
T wo little kittens fooling their mum
E verybody come and play
N ow it's time to go to bed
S leep tight sweet cat!

Carly Insley (9)
Lostock Gralam CE Primary School

The Tiger Kennings

A fierce predator
A sly hunter
A creeping killer
A growling leaper
A cautious prowler
A ferocious eater
A stealthy killer
A ferocious growler.

Connor Preston (10)
Mansfield Primary School

Tiger Kennings

An ear-blasting roarer
A levitating leaper
A stealthy strider
A preaching pouncer
A conniving killer
A hasty hunter
A spectacular spyer
A troublesome tearer.

Rachel Nield (11)
Mansfield Primary School

Tiger Kennings

A high pouncer
A loud growler
A silent hunter
A vicious killer
A speedy runner
An inaudible sleeper
A predator scratcher
A strong tearer
An energetic leaper.

Lois Bowckett (9)
Mansfield Primary School

Shark Kennings

A speedy attacker
A frenzied eater
A ruthless killer
A jagged teeth owner
A man-eating beast
A furious avenger
An attacking artist.

Danielle Williams (10)
Mansfield Primary School

Just Believe . . .

Just believe me all the time.
Just pretend I am a sparkling dime.

Just believe paper clips are bendy
Just pretend you look dead trendy.

Just believe me when I say
Come out, come out, come out to play.

Amy Riches (9)
Mansfield Primary School

My Friend

He is clumsier than a monkey
On a chandelier drinking beer.

He is slower than a slug
On a glue stick in concrete.

He is crazier than Busted
When they win the lottery.

He is fatter than a car
With 60 balls stuck on it.

Kristopher Jones (9)
Mansfield Primary School

My Friends

She is faster than a cheetah
He is slower than a tortoise
She is naughtier than Dennis the Menace
He is colder than a snowman in the snow
She is madder than an ape in the rainforest
He is brainier than God
She is taller than a giant old ogre.

Terri-Ann Hammond (8)
Mansfield Primary School

Bin Bag

Black jelly wobbling on a shaking branch
A rubbish gobbler coming for your trash
A bin's quilt keeping him warm inside
Black ice sliding across the kitchen floor
A white ghost who has just been to a firework display.

Kelly Rochell (11)
Mansfield Primary School

My Friends

He is funnier than Daffy Duck
In a bus.

She is slower than a cheetah
Carrying a hedgehog.

He is faster than a cheetah
Who's hungry for his dinner.

She is clumsier
Than Bugs Bunny.

He is stronger
Than a lion.

Izaac Allmark (8)
Mansfield Primary School

Horse Kennings

A skilful jumper
A friendly trotter
A grass eater
A noise maker
A lovely creature
An apply lover.

Hayley Davies (10)
Mansfield Primary School

Duck-Billed Platypus

A strange creature
A good swimmer
A fussy eater
An egg layer.

Joshua Karl Jones (10)
Mansfield Primary School

Black Panther Kennings

A fierce hunter
A night seeker
A black killer
A speeding runner
A body breaker
An intestine splatterer
A food needer
A life ender.

Shaun Ridge (10)
Mansfield Primary School

Cheetah Kennings

A fast sprinter
   A tense pouncer
      A proud strider
      A determined climber
   A spotty creature
A camouflaged hunter.

Rebecca Weeks (9)
Mansfield Primary School

The Wolf Kennings

A powerful predator
A swift mover
A fast runner
A silent prowler
A skilful attacker
A magnificent leaper.

Jason Horgan (10)
Mansfield Primary School

My Imaginary Friends

He is naughtier than Dennis the Menace
With a chainsaw in a glass factory.

She is colder than an Eskimo in a fridge
With no clothes on in the Antarctic.

She is skinnier than a dog
On a diet in a slim factory.

She is noisier than an elephant
With cymbals.

She is taller than the Twin Towers
On top of each other with stilts.

She is bouncier than Tigger
With springs on his bottom
At the mattress factory on a bungee-jump.

Connor Lenton (8)
Mansfield Primary School

My Friends

She is skinnier than a stick.
He is naughtier than Royson.
She is slower than a tortoise stuck in glue.
He is crazier than a monkey who's seen a hundred bananas.
She is smaller than an ant.
He is taller than a giraffe on stilts.
She is fatter than a pregnant elephant.

Zoe Wojtala Petterson (8)
Mansfield Primary School

Night Of Darkness

October 31st that is the day,
When all things bad come out to play.
So you think it is safe to trick or treat,
When all the ghosts and ghoulies meet.

Just how safe do you think you are?
When you're being watched by eyes not afar.
Taking the treats and enjoying it all,
Whilst the witches chant in their yearly ball.

So children please do be aware,
For you really could be in for a scare.
Those masks and costumes you think are all fake,
Are watching and waiting and ready to take!

Beccy Atherton (9)
Mansfield Primary School

My Friend

He is faster than a car on a race track.
He is angrier than a volcano erupting.
He is taller than a giraffe on stilts.
He is fatter than two elephants stuck together.
He is slower than a snail on super glue.
He is cleaner than a plate that's just been washed in a dishwasher.
He is slimmer than a stick insect on a diet.

Carly Bowckett (7)
Mansfield Primary School

My Friend

He is faster than Michael Owen with his pants on fire.
He is hungrier than a whale that has not eaten dinner in days.
He is lazier than a lion that has just eaten dinner.
He is fatter than an elephant.
He is skinnier than a stick.
He is slower than a tortoise that has just eaten dinner.
He is naughtier than Dennis the Menace with a chainsaw.
He is more dangerous than a baby with an army truck.
He is faster than Michael Schumacher getting chased by a gorilla.

Jordan Elwell
Mansfield Primary School

My Friends

He is taller than the Eiffel Tower on stilts.
He is hotter than the sun in ten million pairs of clothes.
He is crazier than a chimpanzee that's gone bananas.
He is sillier than a hippo in a tutu driving a square-wheeled car.
She is stronger than Jackie Chan who's exercised all year.
He is faster than a cheetah who's being chased by a police car.
He is bouncier than Tigger when he's bouncing on a bouncy castle.
He is faster than a race car speeding away from an elephant.

Lauren Peaurt (9)
Mansfield Primary School

My Friend

He is fatter than fat friends eating junk food.
He is faster than Michael Schumacher in his Formula 1 car.
He is clumsier than a clown on stilts.
He is colder than an Eskimo stuck in ice.
He is slower than a tortoise on ice.

Dean Bennett (9)
Mansfield Primary School

My Friends

He is fatter than two elephants
Stuck together eating a hundred bars of chocolate.

She is colder than a snowman.

He is naughtier than Dennis the Menace
In a tank.

He is slower than a tortoise in a race
Because he was stuck in glue.

Curtis Ledsham (8)
Mansfield Primary School

My Friends

He is funnier than Lenny Henry
With his hat on fire.
She is slimmer than a cat
Drinking beer.
He is angrier than a cat
Being chased by a dog.

Emma Rochell (7)
Mansfield Primary School

My Friend

He is fatter than two elephants stuck together.
He is naughtier than Dennis the Menace
With a chainsaw in a classroom.
He is sillier than someone having fun with a cat.
He is colder than an ice cube In a freezer.

Charlotte Lenton (7)
Mansfield Primary School

My Friends

He is stranger than an alien with a mission gun.
She is naughtier than Dennis the Menace with a hundred daggers.
She is weirder than a flying pig.
He is clumsier than Rudolph the red-nosed reindeer
And Father Christmas drunk on Christmas night
From drinking all the sherry.
She is slimmer than a stick insect on a diet.
She is angrier than a bull
That sees a red packet of beefburgers in a shopping bag.

Samantha Ogden (9)
Mansfield Primary School

My Friends

She is slimmer than a stick insect on a diet.
She is naughtier than Tracy Beaker with a gun in a gas factory.
He is colder than a polar bear at the North Pole.
She is smaller than a mouse having some cheese.
He is crazier than a cat on a tightrope.
He is fatter than a big, fat elephant on a bike.
He is faster than Michael Schumacher drunk.

Claire Atkins (8)
Mansfield Primary School

My Friend

He is fatter than two elephants on top of each other.
He is naughtier than a baby with a shotgun.
He is colder than the North Pole in summer.
He is hotter than Australia all year round.

Jake Jones (7)
Mansfield Primary School

My Friend

He is naughtier than Dennis the Menace
with a machine gun in a glass factory.
He is funnier than Mr Bananas dancing.
He is clumsier than the Twin Towers on roller skates.
He is crazier than Bowser with a chainsaw.
He is slower than a tortoise stuck in super glue.
He is colder than the North Pole.

James Robert O'Regan (8)
Mansfield Primary School

My Friends

She is funnier than a talking tree.
He is bouncier than Tigger.
She is slimmer than a mouse's tail.
He is slower than a turtle on roller skates.
She is taller than Bugs Bunny in an ice cream van.
He is naughtier than Dennis the Menace.

Lucy Sweeney (8)
Mansfield Primary School

My Friend

He is skinnier than a penguin on a diet.
He is colder than a snowman in a freezer.
He is taller than a giant on stilts.
He is brainier than an insect.
He is hotter than fire.

Daniel Longhorn (8)
Mansfield Primary School

Snake Began

Snake began.
He stole the birch bark and the scales of a
Fish and made his skin.

To make his voice he took the fury of
The hail and the hiss of steam.

From the thunderous sky he whisked the
Lightning for his speed and the clouds for agility.

For the sound of his movement he stole the
Rustling of dry grass.

He seized the blackest stones from the
Mines and the iciest stars from the sky
To make his eyes.

For the venom in his fangs he stole cold
Death itself and took the glittering
Sharpness of a dagger.

For his slither he took the movement of
Running water.

For his tongue he took the outline of a tree
Split in half by lighting

And snake was made.

Isabel Wilkinson (10)
Nether Alderley Primary School

Snake Began

Snake began
She took the hiss from the gentle breeze,
She took the stutter from a car engine,
To make her voice.

For her body,
She took the green scales of a crocodile,
The roughness of an old brick wall,
The coldness of a knight's shining armour.

She took the blackness of a blackberry,
She took a piece of the glowing moon
For her eyes.

For her movement,
She took the slither from a slug,
She took the quietness of a snowflake falling.

She took the jump of a frog,
She took the hop from a rabbit,
She took the strike of a cheetah
And made her pounce.

For her tongue,
She took a forked twig,
She took the redness of blood

And the snake was made.

Chloe Venables (10)
Nether Alderley Primary School

Snake Began

Snake began,
He stole the length of the giraffe
And he stole the weight of the elephant,
To make his body.

He stole the chain mail of a knight
And he stole the strength of an ox
To make his scales.

He stole the movement of the worm
And he stole the silence of the dark night sky
To make his slither.

He stole the hiss of a whisper
And he stole the hiss of a cockroach
To make his voice

He stole the point of a spear
And he stole the sharpness of a shark's tooth
For his fangs

And snake was made.

Edward Finch (10)
Nether Alderley Primary School

Snake Began

Snake began,
From the darkness of the moist soil,
From the armour of a knight
And made its scales.

It took its movement
From a cheetah's shadow,
Slick, fast and quiet
And made its agility.

It stole its hiss
From nails on blackboard
And the sound of the waves
And made its hiss.

Its poison was made by
The sting of a wasp
And the venom of a frog,
It made its poison.

And snake was made.

Ross Guirey (11)
Nether Alderley Primary School

Snake Began

Snake began
It took the speed of a whiplash
It took the cold rope of the gallows
And made its body.

For its hood
It stole the cloak of the sky
It took the cool shade of the trees
And the shadow of the night.

Thorns and brambles
And the speed of a dart
It stealthily took
And made its tongue.

Dragon's fire
And the blade of a knife
The tip of an arrow, the last breath of a life,
Made its venom.

For its mind
It took the thoughts of a spy,
The stealth of a fox
And snake was made.

Dylan Sumner (11)
Nether Alderley Primary School

Snake Began

He took the hisses from the angry cat
And stole the silence of the moonlight
And made his hiss

For his scales
He stole the overlapping of clothes folds
And the sleekness of silk

He sneaked the long, thin branch shape
Then put the scales over it

For his predator skills
He chose the quick cheetah
And the quietness of a person who lost their tongue

He took his forked tongue from a split roadway
And the movement he created himself
And made his tongue

Snake was created.

Katherine Reynolds (10)
Nether Alderley Primary School

A Freezing Tale

Snow is a big white blanket
covering the ground

Snowflakes are like diamonds
floating down from the sky

Hailstones are pebbles
battering against your skin

Snow is pearls
drifting from Heaven.

Jemma Hawkes (10)
St Basil's Catholic Primary School, Widnes

On My Way Home

I was on my way home and all I could see was
Snow covering the floor like a giant's blanket,
The snow feels like sinking sand dragging me under the ground,
The wind is like a giant breathing in my face,
The icicles are frozen crystals stuck to my hand,
The grey sky is an elephant's body covering the world below,
The rain is like teardrops from the angels in Heaven,
And the snow is a giant sheep asleep in the fields.

Rebecca Gill (10)
St Basil's Catholic Primary School, Widnes

A Winter Night

I am walking home from school,
I see a tree, it looks like a frozen giant's leg,
The floor is as slippy as a wet, icy slide under my feet,
My arms are colder than ice cubes in the Antarctic,
The snow is a big white blanket that my legs are sinking into,
My scarf is a big warm snake wrapped around my neck,
My jumper is a flock of sheep gathered around to keep me warm,
Winter is the time when the Earth freezes.

James Robertson (9)
St Basil's Catholic Primary School, Widnes

The Winter Night

I am walking home from school and the frost and ice
On my feet is as cold as an ice cube in the Antarctic,
As I climb out of bed, the air that is as cold as an ice bath
Has made my bed freezing,
Out of the window the wind is like a howling werewolf,
I can just feel the hail dropping on my head,
It feels as cold as a frozen penguin,
The ice is like little sparkling lights on the ground,
The ground is slippier than a frozen slide underneath me.

Ryan Smith (9)
St Basil's Catholic Primary School, Widnes

When I Grow Up

When I grow up I'll be a racer
And race to the finish line
Or will I be a digger
And look for gold in a mine?

Will I be a Mayoress
And boss people around
Or will I be a pop star
And make a lovely sound?

Will I be a painter
And be like Vincent Van Gogh
Or will I be a naturalist
And search for the golden moth?

Will I be a sailor
And sail the seven seas?
Actually, I think I'm better off
Me, just being me.

Abigail Irons (9)
St Basil's Catholic Primary School, Widnes

What Am I?

I have black skin, two huge ears that stick out,
I have two round feet and cobwebs dangling from my mouth
And snail trails all over me.
I have smelly dog breath which stink-bombs the whole house out!
But there's no reason why they should hide me away
Just because I stink all day.
Every week my mother comes, so I can regenerate my lovely garbage!
Nonsense! Oh cruel human man keeps me away all day,
You would not want to be me, never seeing the crack of dawn,
Just kept away in a soggy old lawn,
In a cupboard in a garage, this life is just not fair,
Please, instead I'll be just a very black teddy bear,
It's a hard life for me, nobody loves me, what am I?

Rebecca Dwyer (9)
St Basil's Catholic Primary School, Widnes

Winter

My legs, my hands, my feet, my fingers,
They all feel so numb,
The roads look like they're completely gone
Because they are covered in snow,
My scarf is a fluffy snake wrapped all around my neck
And of course my woolly jumper is a fluffy teddy bear,
The leaves of the trees are frozen and like crisps
Because they are really crispy,
The trunk of the trees are a giant's leg that is frozen.

Becky Taylor (9)
St Basil's Catholic Primary School, Widnes

My Dad

My dad is a light like the moon
On a cold winter's night
His place is sitting in his car
Every single night
My dad is a comfy rocking chair
Rocking you to sleep
My dad loves action films
Wondering what's happening next
He is a hot pot on an autumn night.

Kenny Sanderson (11)
St Basil's Catholic Primary School, Widnes

My Dad

My dad is a bright golden sun shining everywhere,
He is a summer shining and he is a bright sun,
My dad is a super man,
My dad is a chocolate cake,
My dad is a very bright star,
My dad is the very bright moon.

Andrew Brookfield (10)
St Basil's Catholic Primary School, Widnes

Autumn Poem

The rain is like one thousand bombs
Dropping on the city,
The fox is a small brush
Mopping up the autumn leaves,
The fog is like the steam from an
Old steam train.

The grass is like a person's hair
Spreading across the city park,
The hedgehog is a spiky ball
Rolling round and round,
The trees are big, green monsters
In the forest.

The sun is like a great ball of fire,
The black autumn berries are round and sweet,
The autumn leaves are the trees having their hair cut,
The ice is freezing cold,
The dinner is really warm,
Just waiting for you!

Chris Barton (11)
St Basil's Catholic Primary School, Widnes

Marvellous Mum

My mum is a shining silver moon
Who tucks me up at night,
She is a winter night with a warm, welcoming heart,
She is a living room with a blazing fire,
She is a swirling whirlpool, polishing all the house,
She is a sparkling new suit with buttons like stars,
She is a warm, cosy bed which feels like a million feathers,
She is the Matrix and as strong as can be,
My mum is a hot toffee pudding covered in cream
And delicious, melted chocolate.

Hannah Conway (11)
St Basil's Catholic Primary School, Widnes

My Fantastic Sister

My fantastic sister is a sun sparkling a bright orange glow,
She is a warm summer afternoon in a countryside in Wales,
She is a happy sunshine, smiling all of the time,
My sister is a funny clown suit, making people laugh,
She is a large, comfy chair that makes people feel welcome,
She is Art Attack, a very creative person,
My fantastic sister is a delicious, pink birthday cake.

Leanne Griffiths (11)
St Basil's Catholic Primary School, Widnes

Winter

The leaves are like rain dropping on the ground
The branches are like a creaky door opening
The tree trunk is a person being frozen
The twigs are like pencil leads
My legs are frozen and my fingers are numb
My scarf is a snake wrapping around my neck
The hat on my head is a bear's hands
Covering my frozen ears.

Lauren Maxwell (10)
St Basil's Catholic Primary School, Widnes

Winter

The fog is a blanket of dust blowing around the air,
The snow is as white as a ghost flying down from the sky,
The hailstones are bullets striking you on the face,
A snowman is a frozen scarecrow standing on guard,
A sledge is a sports car zooming down the hill,
The snow is as crunchy as crisps being munched.

Sam Brittles (9)
St Basil's Catholic Primary School, Widnes

Winter

One winter night my feet are as freezing as a snow shower,
My head is colder than a melted ice cube,
The weather is more terrible than a gale lashing against houses,
The rain is a huge bubble coming from Mars,
My eyes are as watery as a lake,
The trees are bigger than two giant's legs frozen,
The grass is whiter than the whitest snow,
The snow is little ships coming down from space,
The ice is slippier than a watered frozen slide,
My door handle is frozen more than an icy floor,
Wind is a whirlwind with ice in it.

Liam Moores (9)
St Basil's Catholic Primary School, Widnes

Mad Winter

A sledge is a Ferrari speeding 90 miles an hour down the hill,
A snowman is a frozen soldier standing on guard,
A snowball is a gigantic white balloon floating in the air,
A snowball is a shiny crystal ball spinning all over the place,
Fog is a ginormous blanket of dust swishing in the air,
The ground is as white as a polar bear,
The hail is sharp needles rolling from the sky.

Kyle Ruane (10)
St Basil's Catholic Primary School, Widnes

A Cold Frosty Morning

My scarf was like a big anaconda about to bite me,
My big woolly jumper was as thick as a big ball of wool
                                        wrapped around me,
My socks were like a big baboon wrapped around my feet,
My hat was like a big hippo on top of my head,
The trees were like a giant's foot right next to me looking down on me.

Elliott Hamlett (10)
St Basil's Catholic Primary School, Widnes

The Annual Winter Blast

The hail is bombs falling and departing like a million
                                        dropped diamonds,
Roads are never-ending uncoiling snakes in a jungle of
                                        amazingly awesome buildings,
The countryside is a silent, solitary confinement,
The streets are a dismal funeral,
Public places are as lifeless as an ancient graveyard in the
                                        middle of a desert,
Snow and rain rage down like a festival of blue lightning,
Leaves are crunchy bones being squashed by a ferocious giant,
I am running now like a killer on the run from the police,
The sun is gradually rising, it is like the timid mouse peeking for the
cat,
The warmth of my house surrounds me like a comforting
                                        granny embracing me,
Lights shine down, the city is like an alien with nine billion
                                        mouths, unlike the night before,
Winter is an annual, petrifying, dreaded, melancholy, wretched blast.

Sam Argent (10)
St Basil's Catholic Primary School, Widnes

Winter

A snowball is as cold as an ice cube frosted in a freezer,
A snowman is a lamp post standing in the frost,
My uncle's dog is a teddy in an oven,
A polar bear is as white as the floor at Christmas in the North Pole,
My face is as wet as a cat playing in the rain,
My feet are as cold as a storm with hailstones,
My hands are as cold as a polar bear's paw,
My gloves are as wet as the grass,
A scarf is a bonfire trapped in a hot radiator,
The clothes are as warm as a burning fire.

Tom Hunter (10)
St Basil's Catholic Primary School, Widnes

What Am I?

I have black-oloured skin with a tattoo of Avon
And twenty-two on my chest
I am dirty with smelly dog breath
My feet are round
My feet are round
My mouth is closed most of the time
My mouth is opened when you lift my eyes
I can be full, I can be empty
Every Tuesday in the morning I am sick in my mother's belly
She gets taken to the mother of all . . . and she is sick
Most of the time hidden away at the bottom of the garden
Occasionally I swallow my master when he's feeding me!
He feeds me bottles, wrappers, pencil sharpenings and waste food,
Lucky me!
I love the feel of spiders running in my belly,
I live outside
What am I?

Adam Jackson (9)
St Basil's Catholic Primary School, Widnes

What Am I?

I have a large black belly, I am covered in tattoos
And I am camouflaged,
I have two large, bulging, round eyes
Which my master nearly pulls them out of their sockets
In opening my big greedy mouth,
He then enters my scrummy food which I chomp and chomp at
As he walks away,
Whenever I see humans passing by I begin to drool,
I have plastic round legs for my master to push me on,
He takes me to my father and I empty myself into him,
He then trundles home and empties his food onto the floor,
But I do have one fear and that is *water!*
It tortures me until I feel myself burning and then in desperate need
Of food but no one comes.

Christopher Rose (10)
St Basil's Catholic Primary School, Widnes

Ten Little Children

Ten little children
Went to dine
One got lost
Then there was nine

Nine little children
Went to the gate
One got trapped
Then there were eight

Eight little children
Went to Heaven
One got chucked down
Then there were seven

Seven little children
Making a mix
One got splashed
Then there were six

Six little children
Went for a dive
One couldn't swim
Then there were five

Five little children
Sliding on the floor
One fell over
Then there were four

Four little children
Playing with a bee
One got stung
Then there were three

Three little children
Playing at the zoo
One got bit
Then there were two.

Matthew Naylor (9)
St Basil's Catholic Primary School, Widnes

Snowy Morning

I feel the snow falling down at my feet like bombs,
The sky is darker than space with snow making stars,
The cars are frozen like ice,
There is a bus stuck in snow,
The snow is as white as milk,
The floor is like polar bear's skin,
The land is whiter than a polar bear,
The people's clothes look like a bag of candyfloss
And the ground is totally white,
The tree trunks in the country are frozen like giant's legs.

Daniel Saunders (9)
St Basil's Catholic Primary School, Widnes

Winter Clothes

I feel the warmth of my jumper that is as thick
As a chunky piece of wool wrapped all around my body,
My scarf is as spotty as a snake wrapped around my neck,
My socks are mammoth's fur wrapped around my feet,
The ice ring looks like sapphire crystals on the ground,
The sky is like a black piece of coal in the fireplace,
The Wellington boots are umbrellas shielding my feet,
The hailstones are frozen meteors striking at you.

Ben Dourley (10)
St Basil's Catholic Primary School, Widnes

Winter

The mittens on my hands are a fluffy polar bear's hands,
The scarf wrapped around my neck is like a spotty snake,
My hat is a polar bear's fur on my head,
My jumper is like a sheep's wool wrapped around me,
The wellies on my feet are giant's boots stomping on the ground,
My socks are like fifteen pairs of animal skin wrapped around my feet.

William Hughes (9)
St Basil's Catholic Primary School, Widnes

What Am I?

What am I?
I am rustier than a big old tin
Bigger than the stormy sky
It doesn't wear a vest
It slips in the rain, cold and ice
It is as fat as a cupboard door
It gets fed every day
Throws up every week
Gets chucked into a bigger bin than me
As fat as a car
The bees are my bodyguard
The string on me is worse than me
Rolling on a bee that could never happen
Because I have no legs
My feet are round
I have no arms.

Josh McCann (9)
St Basil's Catholic Primary School, Widnes

On My Way Home In Winter

As I walk home I see a giant white velvet blanket
Of snow covering the bed of the countryside,
Where ground was once charred by fire,
Meets the freezing wrath of snow like ice.

The frostbite like being stabbed with
A thousand knives of fire in the stomach,
The sky a frozen sapphire cut flawlessly
By the hands of God under the light of Heaven.

The ice breaks like shattered diamonds,
Broken by Thor's hammer,
The ground is a floating chessboard
And I am merely a pawn.

Daniel Hughes (10)
St Basil's Catholic Primary School, Widnes

What Am I?

I can be coloured, I can be dull
I can be empty, I can be full
My belly is rumbling, my ears can hear
I can't wait because food is near

I can be outside, I can be away
I don't really have time to play
I have feet, but no legs
Sometimes I eat broken pegs

Every Wednesday I am sick -
Into my mum and down with a tick
I can be dirty, I can be clean
I have a bath without being seen

I have a tattoo, I have clothes
I have not got any toes
I have ears and eyes
It is a pity I don't wear ties

What am I?

Martin Maguire (10)
St Basil's Catholic Primary School, Widnes

My Nanna

My nanna is as cheerful as the colour yellow, lighting up my life,
She is a cool breeze on a hot summer's morning
And a shady corner where I can sit,
She is a bright candle, lit in church, praying to God,
She is an orange sun in a heavy shower of rain,
A new pair of brown sandals walking over the long green grass,
My nanna is a comfy armchair with the local newspaper next to it,
She is the one who wins everything on 'The Vault'
And a Sunday dinner with warm gravy spread on top of it,
She is the best nanna in the world and I love her.

Emma Moss (10)
St Basil's Catholic Primary School, Widnes

A Christmas Tree's Christmas

All the excited children
Had faces full of glee
For they had been waiting all year long
And it was Christmas finally

I watched them open their gifts
As they all sat down around me
Toy cars, dolls and teddy bears
What a special sight to see

One child didn't believe
And received only coal
So from then on he promised
To develop a Christmas soul!

My present comes early
Sometimes on Christmas Eve
I get to see Father Christmas
Deliver gifts and then leave

So that was what happened
Upon this Christmas Day
It was fun while it lasted
But now I'm being packed away.

James O'Donnell (10)
St Basil's Catholic Primary School, Widnes

My Uncle

My uncle is a golden sunrise in the early morning
He is the summer morning
He is Twickenham rugby ground
My uncle is a lightning bolt going through the defence to score
He is an England rugby kit
He is a big armchair with some cushions
My uncle is the kids' channel
He is a big pile of homemade chips and eggs.

Simon Buckle (11)
St Basil's Catholic Primary School, Widnes

What Am I?

I have a great fat belly
I am usually black in Holton
I can be full and empty
I have two round feet
I have smelly breath
I have numbers on my back or front
Once a week my food goes into a monster's mouth
I have a lot of brothers and sisters
My food is scrap and rubbish
I can have tattoos
I can be dirty with smelly things inside me
Or I can be clean with lovely things inside me
Like bags or plastic
All year round I eat and eat and eat
I can be hidden so no one hurts me
What am I?

Daniel Roberts (10)
St Basil's Catholic Primary School, Widnes

What Am I?

I am smelly and horrible,
I am camouflaged with numbers,
I am greener than grass,
I live outside in a big garden,
I drink rain when it falls from the sky,
I have my mouth open all day,
I am full of water every weekend,
I am sick in a big van on Wednesday,
I have legs as round as footballs,
I never stop getting fed.
What am I?

Liam Ogburn (10)
St Basil's Catholic Primary School, Widnes

Magical Christmas Eve

That lovely Christmas Eve,
I can never ever wait to leave.
So many gifts and so many toys,
To deliver to all those girls and boys.

The reindeer and sleigh ready to go,
Flying above all that glistening snow.
Rudolph and Prancer, rascals they are,
Never keen on flying far.

Landing on those snowy rooftops,
All the popping up and down, hardly ever stops,
The children fast asleep in bed,
'Hurry up slow coach!' those reindeer said.

I love that special and magical day,
But bit by bit it fades away,
Then I wait just one more year,
'Cause Christmas Eve will reappear.

Thomas Walsh (11)
St Basil's Catholic Primary School, Widnes

What Am I?

My name is Tim, I look like a large tin who could gobble you
Up in a second, I hate it when it rains,
It gives me lots of pains in my eyes
And definitely my nose, I hate it when the slugs
And other kinds of bugs crawl up the left of my back
I hate it when the slime runs down to the bottom of my spine
It makes my black bottom all slippery
I take no chance for wasps and bees
Because they protect me from other living things,
What am I?

Lewis Baines (10)
St Basil's Catholic Primary School, Widnes

Blame

'Hannah, look at Jordan's shoes,
He says you tried to paint them.'
'I did Miss, yes with my paintbrush,
But Alecia told me to do it.'

'Hannah, look at Jack's bag,
It's got a huge hole in it!'
'It was only an experiment with my hole puncher
And Alecia told me to do it.'

'Simon's pencil case is stuck to the table,
Look Hannah, did you glue it?'
'Yes, but I never thought it would work
And Alecia told me to do it.'

'Alecia, what's all this I hear
About you and Hannah Fry?'
'Well Miss, it's really more her fault,
She tells me to tell a lie.'

Alecia McWhirter (10)
St Basil's Catholic Primary School, Widnes

What Am I?

I am scruffy and dirty
I am round and fat
And I have dints in me
I am always hot, cold and dry
I smell and I stay outside all day
I'm metal and I always stay in one place
Boys come knocking me off balance
I get horrible waste, I get lifted up by these horrible machines
They look horrible
I live in a street where no one cleans up
I have rotten bananas in my big tub.

Sean Franey (10)
St Basil's Catholic Primary School, Widnes

Christmas Poem

Christmas comes but once a year,
Where people give presents and get drunk on beer,
When Santa comes it's always a grin,
To find him stuck in the chimney again,
To push and pull and scream and shout,
We can't get 'mince pie eating' Santa out
Good old Rudolph with his big red nose,
Rescues fat Santa by tickling his toes,
Our Santa will not make the same mistake see
Because now he uses a magic key,
Mince pies and carrots we leave out at night,
For Santa never wins, there is hardly a fight,
For mince pies are Rudolph's favourite snack,
Santa eats carrots, he carries the sack,
Full of presents, he brings none back,
People are happy throughout the land,
For Santa makes our favourite sound,
'Ho, ho, ho' is all that we hear
And he disappears for another year.

Gemma Marshall (10)
St Basil's Catholic Primary School, Widnes

What Am I?

What am I?
I'm black and dull placed in a dark corner
I watch the snails and slugs clean me
With their silvery trails
My eyes lay in wait for the incoming intruder
The wasps buzz round inside looking for robbers
I'm as pongy as a sock that hasn't been cleaned for a century
I'm as big as a radiator standing on its corner
I'm as heavy as 64 elephants put together
I have big black feet that make me walk
What am I?

Antony Marshall (9)
St Basil's Catholic Primary School, Widnes

When Christmas Came

Christmas came,
The children built me again,
I had a carrot for my nose,
I had sticks for my toes.

I had a mouth made out of coal,
I held onto a pole,
I had a hat,
I had some kind of scarf on me.

The sun came out,
My hat fell again,
I had no nose,
I didn't have my toes,
Oh no I'm melting again.

Hannah Fry (10)
St Basil's Catholic Primary School, Widnes

What Am I?

I have a large mouth which gets fed every day,
Two round ears,
Two squeaky feet like a mouse,
I also have dog breath,
Wasps protect me and slugs clean me,
If I like I could eat you,
My mum or dad comes once a week,
I am often sick in their mouths,
I have a number tattoo on my belly,
I can be as dirty as mud,
I am hidden away from the rain at night,
Where I am camouflaged among black cats.
What am I?

Alexandra Rathbone (10)
St Basil's Catholic Primary School, Widnes

Silver Star

My mum is like the sky going darker at night, dark blue,
She is a cool gentle breeze through a hot summer's day,
My mum is as calm as a river flowing,
She is as warm and bright as the sun,
My mum is a silk silver star watching over me at night,
She is a big comfortable chair that is really squashy when
you sit on her knee,
My mum is The Bill, always getting to the bottom of things,
She is a double chocolate cake that looks so yummy.

Shaunie Lawton (10)
St Basil's Catholic Primary School, Widnes

My Brother

My brother is an orange sunset,
He is a spring morning,
In a cool breezy field,
He is the rain coming down slowly,
He is a football kit,
A rocking chair moving all the time,
He is a Looney Tune,
My brother is a delicious bite of cake.

Hollie Chadwick (10)
St Basil's Catholic Primary School, Widnes

Winter

A tree trunk is a giant's leg that is frozen,
Leaves are like a piece of crusty burnt toast,
A twig is thinner than a skeleton with a pencil lead inside it,
A branch is as fat as a sumo wrestler that has eaten a
massive ice cube,
When the wind blows the trees it sounds like a creaky door opening,
The ice on the floor is like the skin of a banana.

Jake Larkin (9)
St Basil's Catholic Primary School, Widnes

Big Bro

My brother is a red ball of fire
He is summer where everyone is kind
He reminds me of Spain, funny and joyful
He is nice and sunny, all kind and gentle
He is a clown suit, silly and fun
He is a comfy, bouncy bed
He is a funny episode of Keenan and Kel
My big bro is a pepperoni pizza waiting to be eaten
That is why I love my big bro.

Jessica Roberts (11)
St Basil's Catholic Primary School, Widnes

My Head Teacher

Mrs Douglas is a bright, hot, orange, sunny, summer's day,
She is a cool swimming pool on a scorching day,
She is a breezy autumn sunset fading in the west,
She is one of her smart blue dresses,
She is a very neat and tidy desk,
She is Coronation Street, the main focus on TV,
She is a delicious, super, surprise ice cream with a cherry on top.

Daniel Newall (10)
St Basil's Catholic Primary School, Widnes

Cleaning Elephant

A grey big elephant with a long sucking trunk,
Moving around the room devouring everything in sight,
I drop bits on the floor, he's there sucking them in,
He storms out of his cage to the mess,
Every time you see him, he's getting the job done,
He lets out a magnificent roar,
When he's cleaning the dirt,
When he is full he lets it all out.

Joshua Christopher (10)
St Basil's Catholic Primary School, Widnes

What Am I?

I'm dirty and smelly
And I have a big belly
I have legs and feet
I'm squeaky and coloured
My colour is grey and dark
I have a tattoo
It's big and white
I'm camouflaged at night
I have ears
And dark red eyes
I'm hidden away
I'm cold outside
I feel mice jumping around inside
I have round wheels
I get fed every day
I eat something new
When weeks go by
It tastes better every day
But when every week comes
A monster comes down the dark black road
I'm scared to death
When he tips me upside down
And empties me
Now I'm all on my own
Nothing to chew
Until the next day comes
And I'll be ready
To eat ha, ha, ha, he won't stand a chance
And he will never ever take my food
Or else
I will kill him
But he's very big and I'm very small
So it will be the other way round
Oh well.

Becky Sumner (10)
St Basil's Catholic Primary School, Widnes

What Am I?

I can be vicious at times,
Even though I just sit there,
In the dark corner,
My smell keeps aliens and other things away,
I don't like a lot of light,
For the only light I get
Is when the aliens pull me by my ears
And tip me into the mouth of the king,
Sometimes I cannot resist
Gobbling them up.

My clothes are only small
And I like to keep the webs that lie on my belly
Clean and happy,
I have a dark black cover,
Though my friends have some green and some purple,
But in this area
We're all camouflaged.

I get fed with yummy sweet wrappers
And yesterday's leftover tea,
It comes nicely packaged in a black bag,
My dog breath attracts slugs and snails,
Which help me get clean with their slimy trails
And when they have done their duty,
I gobble them up with no fear
That they will do anything to me,
When I was born
I was tattooed
Which was quite strange,
Because it said,
Halton Borough Council.

Hannah Oldfield (10)
St Basil's Catholic Primary School, Widnes

My Mum

My mum is bright yellow, shining like the sun
My mum is a cool breeze on a summer's day
She is fun and amazing like a theme park
She is a warm glowing fire on a cold day
My mum is a fabulous coat with loads of loving pockets
She is comforting like a cosy couch
My mum is EastEnders
My mum is a delicious chocolate cake.

Emily Pitt (10)
St Basil's Catholic Primary School, Widnes

Cool Cousin

My cousin is a red football card
He is spring, the bounciest person I know
On his holidays under the scorching sun
He is the moon looking down from the sky
He is a pair of football boots with lots of skills with a ball
He is a soft, comfortable armchair
And Peter Kay, he is funny
He is as cool as a lovely ice cream.

Adam Gee (11)
St Basil's Catholic Primary School, Widnes

What Is It?

A pitch is a loud stereo when Liverpool play,
The floodlights light the pitch up like a bright day,
Hopes and dreams bring it alive around May,
When Owen gets to that goal, everyone stands up
And that's when it goes like a stereo,
When they come out,
They sing, 'You'll Never Walk Alone',
It is the home of 'The Reds'.

Tom Hague (11)
St Basil's Catholic Primary School, Widnes

What Am I?

I am a black-coloured monster, lurking in your garden,
My breath smells like rotten veg
And my outer is a complete mess,
My eyes are dirty, my feet squeak
And my belly is just sick,
I have a tattoo, lucky me, it says the number 23,
Every time I am emptied, I have a tingling sensation in my belly
And when I'm full again, the emptying goes on and on,
For another 10.
What am I?

John Wise (10)
St Basil's Catholic Primary School, Widnes

What Am I?

I have a big black body
I have a tattoo on my vest
I have some numbers
You have to feed me every day
And I live outside where the bugs can protect me
Inside and outside I'm usually quite smelly
Unless the elephant trunk washes me every week
I am sick into a monster's cave
That gets taken in and emptied into a messy bedroom.

Jessica Washington (9)
St Basil's Catholic Primary School, Widnes

What Am I?

I am full of something horrible and smelly,
I can be purple or black,
I have webs in my ears that tickle me
Through the dark night,
I have tattoos on my belly which look cool in the day,
Everyone comes out the door,
They always hide me round the corner and push me on the floor,
I have always been forgotten,
I think it's not fair.

Rebecca Gallagher (9)
St Basil's Catholic Primary School, Widnes

What Am I?

I am dirty
And smelly
I have two feet
I am as black as night
And I sleep outside
People feed me
I have a big mouth so I would eat you
I get lonely in the night.

Paige Geoghegan (10)
St Basil's Catholic Primary School, Widnes

Icy Crystal Snow

I see white all around me,
Crystal, fluffy, soft and icy,
Velvet covered blanket, what could it be?
But why can't it be spicy?
I don't know much from she or he,
Now I see it, it looks like rice,
It's cold and gentle, wait and see!

Sabrina Moscati (9)
St Mary's Catholic Primary School, Crewe

Winter

Icy trees
Winter's here
Frosty lanes
Winter's here
Winds howl
Winter's here
Snowflakes fall
Cover the wall
Pearly nights
Winter's here.

Hannah Spencer (10)
St Mary's Catholic Primary School, Crewe

Orange Snow

I wish I had some orange snow
To take away the whiteness
I wish I had some orange snow
No more ghostly shadows
Warm and friendly orange snow
Orange snow like the flowers
Orange snow like the sunset
Topsy-turvy upside down
Orange snow all around.

Natalie Matthews (9)
St Mary's Catholic Primary School, Crewe

Guess Who?

Sheets of white on the ground
No one hears me
On garden walls I lay
Winter winds blow me away
Who am I?

Vicki Perry (10)
St Mary's Catholic Primary School, Crewe

The Runaway

I cannot sleep,
Bags under eyes,
Dreaming about
Curious spies,
Have to let it out
And tell the truth,
Or I am going
To lose my proof,
If it is gone
Then I am left,
With nothing
Forced to thieve and theft,
What will happen
To me if I am
Caught by some curious spy?

Eleanor Simmons (10)
St Mary's Catholic Primary School, Crewe

Snowman

Cold
White
Fat
Plump
Coal for eyes
Carrot for a nose
A twig that makes a smile
A green straw hat
Ripped cardigan
Fluffy scarf
Sticks for useless arms

Who am I?

Martin Viashima (10)
St Mary's Catholic Primary School, Crewe

Frost And Snow

F or now it will snow and snow
R emember to go, go, go
O n all the cold ice and snow
S hould we all stay or go and go?
T he people are stuck in snow

A nd all the trees are different shapes
N ow all smaller
D own the hill on a sledge

S now is all on the hedge
N o one knows where it will be
O ver the hill you will see
W ow! Winter's here.

Marc Waterhouse (9)
St Mary's Catholic Primary School, Crewe

My Snowman Spirit

My snowman spirit is always here,
I will never ever fear,
My snowman spirit will never go,
He will always be here when there's snow.

Snow is the best,
When the snow glows,
Out in the snow,
Water is frozen,
Many children playing
And making snowmen,
Nearly all melted.

Lauren Penketh (10)
St Mary's Catholic Primary School, Crewe

Snow Day

Roly-poly down the hill
Goes Joe and his best mate Bill
Snow is falling everywhere
Even landing in people's hair
Snow is here, snow is there
Look out! A polar bear
People making snowmen
Even making a snow den
Frost bites on your face
Look out! A sledge race.

Elliott Oliver (9)
St Mary's Catholic Primary School, Crewe

Snowman Dan

A sheet of snow
Is on the ground
A sheet of snow
Has been found
A sheet of snow
Has made a man
A sheet of snow
Has made our Dan.

Alex Dopierala (9)
St Mary's Catholic Primary School, Crewe

Flowers

Flowers, flowers, beautiful flowers
They have so many colours and so many powers
The beauty they hold
In the colours so bold
Flowers, flowers, every day
They are included in every Christmas play.

Rhiannon Graham (8)
St Mary's Catholic Primary School, Crewe

We're In Snow

Hey! Ho! We're in snow, off to school we go,
Leaving footprints for others to follow,
But beware of hidden hollows,
Rolling, rolling the icy snow,
Off to school we go,
Making balls to throw,
Just watching it grow,
Squeezing, pounding the icy snow,
Off to school we go.

James Hopley (10)
St Mary's Catholic Primary School, Crewe

Snow Everywhere

Snow, snow everywhere
Look out!
A polar bear on the prowl
Snow, snow everywhere
Look around now
Snow, snow everywhere
Look up
Catch a snowflake on your tongue
Quickly, the snow has gone.

Joshua Mellor (9)
St Mary's Catholic Primary School, Crewe

Snow, Ice, Frost

Everywhere is icy
At night have something spicy
Frost, freaky frost
I wish it would defrost!

Ciaran Marks (9)
St Mary's Catholic Primary School, Crewe

Autumn And Winter

Crispy leaves fall to the ground
Not a single green leaf to be found
Every tree wraps up warm and tight
In a big thick coat of shining white

Wrinkly leaves collect in a heap
Like children inside their cosy bed sheets
Badgers hibernate in their straw-ridden setts
And the sparrows fly away from where the ice threats

But now the snow is drifting
The crunching ice is shifting
The powerful winds are leaving
Because spring is on its way.

Siân Manfredi (9)
St Mary's Catholic Primary School, Crewe

From The Snow's View

Snow, snow
Everywhere
With some
Shivering air
Daggers falling
Everywhere
Snow, snow
Everywhere.

Jason Hodgson (9)
St Mary's Catholic Primary School, Crewe

The Snow Poem

Children hiding,
Snowballs flying,
People crying,
Teachers smiling.

Snowing sky,
Birds fly,
Wet sleet,
Cold feet.

Samantha Patrick (9)
St Mary's Catholic Primary School, Crewe

My Pets

Tatty the rabbit in the garden,
She is tatty because her fur is hardened,
She sits in her hutch all day long,
Until we come out singing a song.

Topsy the cat,
Acts like a rat,
He eats his tea and falls asleep,
Then comes downstairs without a peep.

Sooty the puppy is rather fat,
He sits around upon his mat,
Sooty the puppy is very funny,
He hops about like he's a bunny.

All my pets mean a lot to me,
Even when I'm making a cup of tea,
If my rabbit, or cat, or puppy were to ever go missing,
Surely I would be very unhappy.

Lisa Wild (11)
St Peter's RC Primary & Nursery School, Stalybridge

The Old Work Horse

Clip-clop, clip-clop,
Go the hooves of the old work horse,
Ploughing fields, pulling carriages,
People always take Joey for granted,
Never thank him, never treat him,
Yet he goes on working, those long hard hours.

Clip-clop, clip-clop,
Go the hooves of the old work horse,
Along the path,
Past the farmhouse,
To the grand old house,
The old work horses,
Grand old house.

Clip-clop, clip-clop,
Go the hooves of the old work horse,
Into the stable, the grand old house,
Goes in, flops down in the hay,
Realises he's more tired than ever before,
His head droops,
Into the hay,
Never to be lifted again.

Shannon Gilmore (11)
St Peter's RC Primary & Nursery School, Stalybridge

People In My Family

This is Mum who likes to shop
She always buys a lollipop

This is Daniel my small brother
Us two care about each other

This is Dad a very good cook
And often he will read a book

This is Nan who cooks some food
Please be polite, not very rude.

Joseph Lowe (7)
St Peter's RC Primary & Nursery School, Stalybridge

Nature Is Beautiful

Nature is beautiful, so stand still and have a little stare,
For nature is beautiful and it's everywhere,
Even when autumn comes and trees become bare,
Nature is still changing, it's always there.
As leaves fall down from the sky,
Children make piles and try to make them high,
Nature is beautiful so stand still and have a little stare,
For nature is beautiful and it's everywhere,
But in winter it changes again,
Water turns to ice and people make snowmen,
Snowboards very quickly sell out of shops,
Kids put snow in the house, mums get out the mops,
Nature is beautiful so stand still and have a little stare,
For nature is beautiful and it's everywhere,
Summer and spring are the best when everything's green,
When children get out water guns, mums aren't very keen,
The sun shines down in rays of gold,
People take off jackets because it's not cold,
Nature is beautiful so stand still and have a little stare,
For nature is beautiful and it's everywhere.

Daniela Agnello (11)
St Peter's RC Primary & Nursery School, Stalybridge

My Family

This is my mum who goes to the shop
And she buys a big lollipop

This is my dad who is very strong
And he never does things wrong

I have a brother called Bradley
And he goes to bed very sadly

This is my sister called Anna
And she always plays games with my nanna.

Louis Ridgway (7)
St Peter's RC Primary & Nursery School, Stalybridge

My Diary

Dear Diary,
Today was weird, Mum was green and Dad was blue
Kerry went crazy and Andy ate maggots
For his breakfast. Yuck! Weird!

Dear Diary,
Today dead, dead crazy,
Our teacher wasn't in,
So we went home,
We stayed in a castle all night long
And had worms for tea. Eww! Crazy!

Dear Diary,
Today we went on a school trip,
There was a big explosion,
Everyone was OK though,
When it came to lunch, everyone had maggots,
Worms and spiders plus green goo for a drink,
What's going on because I think people
I know are . . .
Aliens!

Adele Murphy (10)
St Peter's RC Primary & Nursery School, Stalybridge

My Family

This is my mum who always shops
She always buys loads of pop

This is my dad who cannot bake
He never eats biscuits, sweets or cake

This is my gran who reads books
She doesn't know any good cooks

This is my brother, Sam, who misspelt 'exam'
His best friend is called Black Dan.

Maxwell Burton (8)
St Peter's RC Primary & Nursery School, Stalybridge

Nutter In Space

The moon's a great big football,
The sun's a pound of butter,
My head is going round the twist
And I'm a little nutter.

Mars is my favourite chocolate bar,
Pluto's a cartoon star,
My head is going round the twist
And I'm a little nutter.

Saturn's got a lovely pattern,
Earth is where I live,
My head is going round the twist
And I'm a little nutter.

Now you've seen the solar system,
How we will miss it,
My head is going round the twist
And I'm a little nutter.

Nathan Cox (10)
St Peter's RC Primary & Nursery School, Stalybridge

The Scorpions Are Running

The scorpions are running
Through the sand
And stinging people
In every land
Its prey is small
Its prey is big
And snapping through the enormous twigs
Then *snap!*
Its clipping claws
Then snap shut
Around a baby human's foot
The baby, oh how she cried
And two hours later . . .
She died!

Jack Luby (10)
St Peter's RC Primary & Nursery School, Stalybridge

Seasons Moan

Winter's the worst,
Summer brightens up the day,
Winter's the worst,
Spring's a breeze.

Winter's the worst,
Autumn's leaves are colourful,
Winter's the worst,
Snow, rain and hail.

Spring brings new flowers,
Summer brings heat,
Spring brings new flowers,
Autumn's nice and cool.

Summer's too hot,
Autumn's kite time,
Summer's too hot,
Winter's too cold.

Autumn's a chill,
Winter's skating time,
Autumn's a chill,
Spring brings sun.

Spring's hay fever time,
Summer's roasting time,
Autumn's messy hair time,
Winter's numb fingers time.

All in all, the seasons are great, except for
Spring, summer, autumn and winter!

Lisa Sweeney (11)
St Peter's RC Primary & Nursery School, Stalybridge

Fruit In A Fruit Basket

Apples they go crunch,
Bananas they go slush,
Coconuts go smash,
While dates they go chew
And grapes go squash.

Fruit is glorious,
Some are nice,
But some are not,
Fruit can be squashy,
While some can be hard.

Kiwi is soft,
While oranges go mushy,
Melon is hard,
Pears go very mushy
And peach goes soft.

People like fruit,
Some people hate fruit,
Fruits are juicy,
Some are sour,
Some fruits have no taste at all.

Strawberries are nice,
Tomatoes they are red,
Lemons are sour,
While berries are squashy
And pineapples are hard.

Fruit can be nice,
Fruit can be bad,
People shout, 'Lovely fruit.'
While we shout, 'Oh no.'
But most of all, fruit is healthy!

Charlie Morton (11)
St Peter's RC Primary & Nursery School, Stalybridge

Cats And Dogs

Cats jump up trees
And dogs run around.
Cats play with keys
And dogs leave mess on the ground.

Cats make kittens,
Dogs chase cats.
Cats play with mittens
And dogs don't wipe their feet on mats.

Cats run away from dogs
And dogs don't like bats.
Cats think dogs are hogs,
Dogs definitely don't like cats.

Cats always like their food,
Dogs have big claws.
Cats' toys are mostly chewed
And dogs have vicious jaws.

Tom Mulholland (11)
St Peter's RC Primary & Nursery School, Stalybridge

The Unicorn, The Fairy And The Elf

Unicorn,
Its snowy white coat shines in the snow,
Its golden horn sparkles in the day,
Its sparkling eyes light up in the night sky.

Fairy,
The beautiful and delicate wings glide through the air,
They can also be lucky or bad or good,
So small like an ant.

Elves,
They are small but smart,
They are lucky but stuffy,
They are like all the rest, they don't exist.

Ben Storey (11)
St Peter's RC Primary & Nursery School, Stalybridge

Environment

People kill,
People kill trees, homes, homes of animals,
The environment is losing this desperate struggle,
People don't care,
Air is polluted,
Animals die,
People don't care,
Plants are dying,
The world is losing control,
People don't care,
Trees are being killed because of us.

David Kempster (10)
St Peter's RC Primary & Nursery School, Stalybridge

My Family

This is my mum she has long hair
When I'm sad, she's always there
This is my sister she is called Sue
And always knows what to do
This is my brother To
And he knows where to go
My dad is strong
And he likes to sing lots of songs.

Daniel Cox (8)
St Peter's RC Primary & Nursery School, Stalybridge

My Family

This is my mum who has long hair
Whenever I'm sad she's always there

This is my brother, Louis is his name
He likes to play PlayStation games.

Cameron McDonald (7)
St Peter's RC Primary & Nursery School, Stalybridge

Animals, Tools And Fruits Of The Alphabet

A is for apple, crunchy and sweet.
B is for bee, busy and buzzy.
C is for cat, clever and cute.
D is for dog, humble and wise.
E is for elephant, large and not scared.
F is for fox, sneaky and sly.
G is for goat, running and skipping.
H is for hippo, lazy and sloppy.
I is for imp, naughty and mean.
J is for jaguar, roaring and purring.
K is for kangaroo, hopping and jumping.
L is for lion, brave and bold.
M is for monkey, cheeky and naughty.
N is for nocuous, shy and hiding,
O is for octopus, slow and important.
P is for python, quiet and surprising.
Q is for quana, fiery and bad-tempered.
R is for rat, horrible and smelly.
S is for shark, fast and speedy.
T is for toucan, soaring and diving.
U is for unicorn, legendary and shy.
V is for vulture, blinding and scary.
W is for whale, gliding and huge.
X is for X-ray, see and seeing.
Y is for yo-yo, forwards and back.
Z is for zebra, galloping and trotting.

Antonio San José (10)
St Peter's RC Primary & Nursery School, Stalybridge

When I Grow Big

When I grow big,
I want to fly,
Even higher than the birds,
I will soar high in the sky.

When I grow big,
I want to act,
I'll go to the audition,
I'll get picked and that's a fact.

When I grow big,
I want to be a teacher,
I'll boss people about,
Nah! Instead I'll be a preacher.

When I grow big,
I'll be a dad,
I'll have a little boy,
I'll always make him so glad.

When I grow big,
I'll be an author,
Writing about adventures,
Flying away in a saucer.

When I grow big,
I want to be me,
Going to school every day,
Getting jealous of teachers drinking tea!

Antony Di-Fruscia (11)
St Peter's RC Primary & Nursery School, Stalybridge

I Have To Go To War

I have to go to war
Or, please Mrs Gaw
It is the law
A war is coming
War is worse than your humming
The house is for let
Oh, I'll have to go, you bet!

I'm at the camp
My bed is damp
I'm a lady
My lamp is fading

Bang, bang, shoot, shoot
Arrrgghh! 1 . . . 2 . . . 3!
Bang!

Rebecca Simonaitis (10)
St Peter's RC Primary & Nursery School, Stalybridge

Starting School

I was four years old,
As good as gold,
I started school,
I thought it was cool.

When I was five,
I was very alive,
I was learning to write,
But couldn't get it right.

Art was fun,
I painted a sun,
I broke friends,
But I made amends.

Bethany Austin (10)
St Peter's RC Primary & Nursery School, Stalybridge

The Dragon Who Had Two Heads

There was a dragon from Dundee,
Who had a huge pear tree,
He had two heads
And three big beds,
He's a terrible sight to see.

His friend was Toole the witch,
Who had a football pitch,
They played together,
In terrible weather
And got the worse kind of itch.

His other friend was Yog,
Who had a big, sticky bog,
He washed his face
At a slow pace
And dried himself with a log.

Siobhan Fairclough (10)
St Peter's RC Primary & Nursery School, Stalybridge

Seasons In The Sun

'We had joy, we had fun, we had seasons in the sun'

It was fun in the sun, in the waves,
It was sad in the snow, in the park,
It was simple in the spring, in the field,
It was awful in the autumn, in the orchard.

'We had joy, we had fun, we had seasons in the sun'

We swam in the sun, in the heat of the summer,
We sledged in the snow, in the cold of the winter,
We had picnics in the meadow, in the warmth of the spring,
We played in the leaves, in the wind and rain of the autumn.

'We had joy, we had fun, we had seasons in the sun'.

Harry Moore (10)
St Peter's RC Primary & Nursery School, Stalybridge

Sport Rhyme

Tennis and football do not rhyme,
But if you want to watch it, it'll cost a dime,
Volleyball and beach ball are basically the same,
But if you say it rhymes, you should feel ashamed,
When you're playing football, the ball goes in the net
And when it's pounding with rain you're surely to get wet;
When the ball is flying,
All our hopes are dying,
Because we know we're not going to win,
But if we do, I'll throw myself in a bin,
So now you know most sports don't rhyme,
But if they say they do, make them eat a lime,
Sorry folks we've run out of time,
But remember, always come to me if you want to rhyme.

Christopher Greenhalgh (10)
St Peter's RC Primary & Nursery School, Stalybridge

If Friends Were Flowers

If my friends were flowers,
I would pick them for sure.
I would pick a bluebell for Daniella
Because of her bright blue eyes.
Vicky a rose, because she is pretty and kind,
Hannah a daisy, because she is always around,
Chloe a lily, because she shows off,
Kayleigh a leaf, because she is light,
Such friends are hard to find
And my friends are one of a kind.

Amy Ashton (10)
St Peter's RC Primary & Nursery School, Stalybridge

Get Me Out Of Here

I went in an old house
And saw one little mouse,
It wasn't a frightening scene,
Then I heard somebody scream,
I wondered what it could be,
Could it be the loud calls from the horrid sea?
I wondered, I wondered.

I went down the creepy hallway,
'This is the creepiest house ever' I did say,
I could hear the creaky floor,
Then by itself something opened the door,
I went through the door so silent and quiet,
Then I saw a big woman who said she's on a diet,
It was creepy, it was creepy.

I went out of the door as quick as light,
So the woman was out of sight,
I went up the stairs to see a window, so I could jump out,
Then I saw somebody coming, it looked like an old trout,
Getting scary, getting scary.

The old trout came in the room and said, 'I need a rest,'
So he took all his clothes off, even his vest,
I got out under the bed and I looked at the old trout
And shouted, '*Argh!* He's naked!'
That's scary, that's scary.

I ran down the stairs,
Which sounded like bears,
Then I ran out of the house to go to the phone,
Just to tell my mum I'm going home.

Conor Trueman (11)
St Peter's RC Primary & Nursery School, Stalybridge

Fairy Land

A fairy here,
A fairy there,
A single fairy everywhere.
A flower here
And over there,
Everything is everywhere.

Flossy, Annie and Clarabell,
Playing together very well.

A tree house here,
A tree house there,
A single tree house everywhere.
There's a wand here
And over there,
Everything is everywhere.

Everybody welcomes you,
Hope your best friends can come too.

Kathleen Lister (10)
St Peter's RC Primary & Nursery School, Stalybridge

My Family

This is Mum, she likes to shop
And she likes to buy some pop

This is Dad who goes to meets
When he comes, he goes and greets

This is Euan, my baby brother
And he is a big lover

This is Cally, my old, old cat
She really does like to chase a rat.

Hannah Welsh (8)
St Peter's RC Primary & Nursery School, Stalybridge

Teachers' Game

The teachers are in the staffroom
Having a break from us,
Moaning, groaning and all sorts,
Making a very big fuss.

Our teacher drops a hot cross bun
Onto another's leg,
She throws one back,
With a great big smack and
'Stop it!' says the head.

The end of this is funny,
We came back into class,
Our teacher was so messy,
She said she'd been to Mass!

Georgia Curley (9)
St Peter's RC Primary & Nursery School, Stalybridge

My Family

This is Mum who has a shop
And wets the floor with a mop
This is my dog who likes a frog
I really, really like my dog
This is my dad who is very strong
And always, always has a song
This is my sister who is cool
She always goes in the pool.

Katie Bowers (8)
St Peter's RC Primary & Nursery School, Stalybridge

School

Up in the morning, off to school
The teacher's making another rule

In the staffroom tea and coffee
The head teacher likes it all frothy

Children playing on the pitch
Out of the classroom comes a witch

She shouts the children into class
'Now,' she shouts, 'we're going to Mass'

Mass is finished, out to play
Children pray for the end of the day

End of the day, teachers wave bye
They get in their car with a very big sigh.

Annie Marshall (10)
St Peter's RC Primary & Nursery School, Stalybridge

My Family

This is my mum who has short hair
Whenever I am sad, she is always there

This is my sister who is tall
When I am glad we play ball

This is my brother called Chris
When I am asleep he makes a hiss

This is my dad who is strong
And he sticks out his tongue.

Alex Danko (8)
St Peter's RC Primary & Nursery School, Stalybridge

My Family

Grandad tries to make me laugh
Sometimes it never works
He is joyful, silly, happy and a bit snappy.

Dad is not that bad . . .
He is okay when he has 70's music on
Dad goes crazy when Man City scores.

Baby Thomas is a little machine
Which never switches off
Already started walking, only just talking.

Mum's working all day long
When she comes home everyone shouts, 'Hooray!'
She is so fast at doing things
Sometimes I think she is Supermum.

Joseph Garside (10)
St Peter's RC Primary & Nursery School, Stalybridge

My Family

This is my mum who loves to shop
And dances round with a mop

This is my brother Ben
Who likes to act like a hen

This is my grandma who bakes
But never likes to steal cakes

This is my dad who is bad
He is always very, very glad.

Heather Watson (8)
St Peter's RC Primary & Nursery School, Stalybridge

My Friend

I have a friend who's really funny,
I have a friend who's cute as a bunny,
I have a friend who's bouncy and black,
I have a friend who's as clear as my dad,
She's very cool and very hot,
She has loads of fur, in fact, *a lot!*
She loves cheese and crackers,
She eats them a lot,
She cooks them herself, in a great big pot,
She smells of perfume, she sprays it on every day,
This horse is so clever,
She's fun in every way.

Holly Gummersall (10)
St Peter's RC Primary & Nursery School, Stalybridge

My Teeth And My Food

Oh how much I love Mum's cakes,
I eat them by the sunny lakes.

Oh how much I love chocolate spread,
I eat it when I'm safe in bed.

Oh I eat a lot of cake of course,
When I am wide awake.

Oh how much I love roast beef,
Hooray! Now I have healthy teeth!

Siobhan-D'Arcie Holden (8)
St Peter's RC Primary & Nursery School, Stalybridge

Rubbish

Rubbish! Rubbish!
Rubbish everywhere!
It twirls and whirls
But it does not care
Bins are out
Bins are in
But it throws it back out again!
It goes out to the street
And back in again
So pick it up
And put it in the bin
But rubbish you can't beat
Rubbish!

Thomas Burgess (10)
St Peter's RC Primary & Nursery School, Stalybridge

Teeth And Food

I really like some jam
I like it better than ham
I am always in a good mood
When I eat some yummy food
I really like roast beef
But it isn't good for my teeth
My dad eats salty chips
But now he licks his lips
My mum likes chocolate spread
And now I have locked it in the shed.

James Garside (7)
St Peter's RC Primary & Nursery School, Stalybridge

Cheetah's Tale

The cheetah runs,
The cheetah eats,
The cheetah sleeps,
The cheetah roars,
The cheetah runs across the plains,
Looking, when it jumps, like it is gliding,
When the cubs of the cheetah are eating,
They look like little bubbles, rising once they have got a mouthful,
When the mother cheetah keeps watch,
She is like a statue, not moving a muscle,
When the little cubs are born,
They miaow and stay cuddling their mum for a long time.

Kerry Angus (10)
St Peter's RC Primary & Nursery School, Stalybridge

My Family

This is my mum who has long hair
When I get hurt she is always there

This is my puppy, her name's Tess
When we leave her muzzle off, she makes a mess

This is my sister, Beth is her name
'Doreen's Day Out' is her favourite game

This is my uncle, his name is Mike
Sometimes he helps me to mend my bike.

Bradley Lewis (7)
St Peter's RC Primary & Nursery School, Stalybridge

Me As Wind

If I were wind
I'd be a terrible force
Screaming and howling
All night long

Grabbing hats and floating bags
I can do all this because I am wind
But if I was myself
I wouldn't have fun
So I'll just stay as wind.

Kane Carty (10)
St Peter's RC Primary & Nursery School, Stalybridge

Dogs Are Great

People say dogs are man's best friend,
Even though they drive you round the bend.

Dogs are sweet and dogs are cute,
So I hope you can play a flute.

Dogs are very cuddly,
Pups are very fiddly.

So get a dog very quick,
Or you will regret it!

Robert Raymond (9)
St Peter's RC Primary & Nursery School, Stalybridge

Africans

Africans wiggle their bum,
To the beat of the drum,
They twirl around
And tap their bum.
Africans dance and sing
All day long,
They clap to the
Beat of the drums,
As they wiggle their bum,
Lord, praise them in every way.

Meagan Taylor (9)
St Peter's RC Primary & Nursery School, Stalybridge

Sport

Sport is hard like football with a ball
Basketball with a basket
Rugby with a post
Sailing with a mast
Curling with a brush
Discus with a disc
Running with a track
Horseracing with a horse
So you see, sport is hard.

Ryan Connor (9)
St Peter's RC Primary & Nursery School, Stalybridge

Leaves In Autumn

The autumn leaves were all around
Brown, brown and yellow on the ground
The leaves were dancing high above
Doing the best they possibly could
Crunching, crunching when you walk
When you open your mouth to talk
A lovely thing comes rushing out
The mist is lingering about

In the sunlight warm, calming
The leaves are silver and very charming
When the leaves fall off the tree
The children will shout 'Whee'
On the floor the leaves disappear
Autumn time is so weird
When the children run, skip and jump
Then all of a sudden there is a big bump

The nights are getting colder
And the sun is going down
The days are getting colder
So we wrap up like a folder
Then we curl up in bed
And fall fast asleep

The moon is waking up
And the dawn is going to bed
Everybody is asleep
Curled up in bed.

Aimee Bates (10)
Shavington Primary School

Autumn's Coming

The autumn breeze ran through the air
And blew the leaves until they danced.
The trees grew close and waved their leaves
And on the windows the frost pranced.

Crunch, crunch, as the leaves were tearing,
Drip, drip, drip, as the dewdrops fell.
Now the sun is shining through,
All the children venture out.

The animals make their last collections,
Robins, rabbits and some wrens.
Scurry off towards their dens,
Ready for the chilly winter.

Now the sun has started to settle,
Birds sing their very last song.
Children tucking into bed,
Ready for another autumn day.

Ellie Hill (10)
Shavington Primary School

The Autumn Breeze

The crispy leaves on the ground and the wind whistling
                                    down the road,
The trees are throwing the leaves at me,
Then the trees go back to sleep,
All the leaves huddle up like at a rugby match,
All the squirrels are rolling nuts around getting ready for hibernation,
The badgers look for some leftovers around the streets,
When it rains, it sits around for the whole season,
When hibernation is over, thankfully autumn and its cold
                                    wind go away.

Sam McKay (11)
Shavington Primary School

Not That It Cared

Ye olde autumn,
The leaves are falling day and night,
While the wind roars like a lion,
It sometimes gives you a fright!

The leaves are sprinting through the air,
While the wind gets stronger and faster,
Getting nastier and nastier,
Now people are scared,
Growing louder and louder,
Not that it cared.

The trees are bending down to their roots,
Snapping branches,
Smashing windows,
When will it ever stop!
Not that it cared.

Matthew Price (10)
Shavington Primary School

Room For Nonsense

Under a spreading Gliptop tree
The village Mulploro stands;
The prom a mighty kro is he
With large and pup hortop hands;
And the muscles of his grofe arms
Are strong as grondale bands.

Week in, week out, from curot to curot
You can hear his purchip group
You can hear him swing his bulgo cruwn
With a measured grou and prout
Like a mupcort ringing the village Gout
When the groutop cropt is low.

Sophie Beeston (10)
Shavington Primary School

The Tired Autumn

'Twas autumn, the dreary one, following the heat of
Summer and leading into the cold of winter.
Oh autumn, the boring one, following summer, the
Lively one and leading winter, the merry one.
Autumn, the grumpy one, following summer, the
Happy one and leading into winter, the friendly one.
Autumn, the slouching one, following summer,
The marching one and leading into winter, the shivering one.
Is autumn just tired?

Sam Bishop (11)
Shavington Primary School

Fire

I was born in the coal and ashes,
My families are burn and flicker,
I live in the hotness of the streaking flames.
I wear a wrap of orange skin and a flaming body,
I am as old as the ashes burnt to death,
I dread the water and cold air surrounding me,
I love the tickle of paper burning inside me, crinkling, burning . . .
Burning . . . *away!*

Daniel Gray (10)
Shavington Primary School

The Raging Sea

The raging sea beats the sand,
The raging sea thrashes about,
The raging sea hits the cliff like a rhino charging into it,
The raging sea's white horses thud on the sand,
The raging sea bites away at the land,
The raging sea still going strong . . .
The raging sea never sleeps.

Tom Edge (10)
Shavington Primary School

Autumn

I once went out to play,
It was a beautiful snowy day.
I felt the air's breath on my face,
I thought: what a wonderful place.
The snow was walking,
The trees were talking,
What wonderful kind of day,
A day to come out and play.

I once went out to play,
It was a beautiful sunny day.
I felt the air's breath on my face.
I thought: what a wonderful place.
The ground was breathing,
The plants were sneezing,
What a wonderful kind of day,
A day to come out and play.

I once went out to play,
It was a beautiful autumn day.
I felt the air's breath on my face.
I thought: what a wonderful place.
The wind was singing,
The leaves were ringing,
What a wonderful kind of day,
A day to come out and play.

I once went out to play,
It was a beautiful spring day.
I felt the air's breath on my face.
I thought: what a wonderful place.
The buds were chatting,
The branches were clatting,
What a wonderful kind of day,
A day to come out and play.

Timothy Gallagher (10)
Shavington Primary School

Autumn End

'Twas a clear autumn night and the sky was awake
As the stars danced over the rippling lake,
Cold fingers of frost added their icy touch
And the lake froze entirely, in the night's frosty clutch.

Autumn fought winter through her veil of mist,
She beat her more closely than she could have wished.
The golden-brown chestnut leaves danced in her breath
For the victory, now that the winter had left.

But alas! Quite unnoticed, the winter crept in!
She rattled around, made a terrible din!
She jumped up at autumn, took her by surprise
And finally led her to her demise!

So winter was queen and autumn had gone,
She had fought bravely, but what's done is done.
The clouds shed tears from high above,
Which frosted to snow, as white as a dove.

Goodbye to clear autumn nights, no longer awake,
No dancing stars over the rippling lake,
The fingers of frost would not lose their cold touch,
So the lake was forever in the frozen ice clutch.

Rebekah Phillips (10)
Shavington Primary School

Sunshine

I was born in the depths of space reaching out with my bright light,
My family are electricity, fire and the yellow of the sun,
I live in the blue sky, moving . . . moving round the world.

I cloak myself in yellow and orange making shadows disappear,
I'm older than the world, stars, even the moon,
I dread the dark, shadows, damp and the cold bringing everyone fear,
I love light, dryness and the warmth in people's hearts.

Stephanie Verstraten (10)
Shavington Primary School

Room For Nonsense

Under a spreading clotthouse tree
The village Lipstack stands;
Thescop a mighty hib is he
With large and tik a pock hands;
And the muscles of his snack boo arms
Are strong as macktoo bands.

Week in, week out, from tirr to hink
You can hear his sing far dink
You can see him swing his wilto hock
With a measured fong and stip
Like a hickbone ringing the village gofe
When the purber fip is low.

Stephanie Sheer (10)
Shavington Primary School

France

F rench people love their posh shopping centres
R omance is at Paris
A eroplanes take an hour to get to France
N etherlands are near to France
C heese is very popular in France
E iffel Tower is over 300 metres high.

Jack Armstrong (8)
Sir John Offley CE (VC) Primary School

France

F rance is fun, it's a very big place
R omance is always happening in France
A rt is what French people always like to do
N ear England is France
C ycling is what children and parents do for a day out
E iffel Tower is 300 metres high.

Ruby Nimbley (8)
Sir John Offley CE (VC) Primary School

Australia

A ustralia is extremely big
U nexpected weather
S ee all of the different places
T ravel everywhere all over it
R oaring animals in the jungle
A ustralia is so hot
L ie on the beach
I like Australia
A ustralia is the best.

Christopher Beech (10)
Sir John Offley CE (VC) Primary School

France

F rance is a big country
R ead means 'lire' in French
A eroplane means 'pavion' in French
N umbers in the French language are different
C apital of France is Paris
E leven million foreign tourists flock to France.

Gemma Haysted (8)
Sir John Offley CE (VC) Primary School

France

F un in France on holiday times
R ich people go shopping in France
A lot of people go to Paris
N ear to France is Spain
C hildren are happy in France
E arly in the morning people go swimming.

Lucy Law (8)
Sir John Offley CE (VC) Primary School

Australia

A koala's fur is very soft
U nder the sun the kangaroos pounce
S izzling and burning on a Christmas Day
T he animals are catching the food for tonight
R ocks as beautiful as Ayres Rock
A boriginal people singing and dancing in the sun
L izards leaping like kangaroos
I t catches your eyes with the frying sun
A boriginal art will look stunning upon your walls.

Charlotte Glover (10)
Sir John Offley CE (VC) Primary School

France

F rench people are famous for wine
R abbits are eaten at Christmas time
A t work are the French on normal days
N ormally they have festivals in a jolly way
C heese they're famous for, carrots they're not
E iffel Tower is very, very hot.

Emily Law (8)
Sir John Offley CE (VC) Primary School

France

F rench people have loads of fun at Christmas
R ain in France doesn't happen very often
A lot of people eat cheese and wine in France
N antes is a place in France
C apital of France is Paris
E iffel Tower is in a part of Paris.

Lori Ward (8)
Sir John Offley CE (VC) Primary School

Australian Animals

A mazing animals lurking around
U nder the trees not a sound
S limy snakes slithering slowly
T aking life almost wholly
R unning fast from the dangers behind
A nd not all animals can be kind
L eaping frogs everywhere
I nside buildings do beware
A nts roaming across the logs
N ever forget about fierce dogs.

Leigh Kontic (11)
Sir John Offley CE (VC) Primary School

France

F rench people eat frogs' legs and snails
R ich people have lots of vineyards
A nd they make tables with nails
N ice people live in France
C ities in France are quite big
E uros in France are their currency.

Ethan White (9)
Sir John Offley CE (VC) Primary School

France

F rench people have vineyards
R omans attacked France
A nd grapes are used for wine
N early 3 million people live in Paris
C roissants are eaten for breakfast
E iffel Tower is very big.

Georgina Hartshorn (9)
Sir John Offley CE (VC) Primary School

Australia

A ustralia is very hot
U nseen land where the animals run
S ee all of the places in Australia
T ravel all over the land
R oaring dingoes in a jungle
A ustralia is very huge
L ie on the beach and relax
I like Australia
A nimals running in the jungle.

Paul Machin (10)
Sir John Offley CE (VC) Primary School

France

F rance is the world's fourth largest producer of cars
R ivers in France you can see
A sterix and Obelix are in comics in France
N euf is the number 9 in France
C heese is famous in France
E ngland is very near to France.

Alex Dracup (9)
Sir John Offley CE (VC) Primary School

France

F un and games are in France
R ace to France to eat their cheese
A rt is famous in France
N ice is a city in France
C apital of France is Paris
E iffel Tower is in Paris.

Corey Doig (8)
Sir John Offley CE (VC) Primary School

The Aussie Awards

Here comes Kylie the kangaroo
With her little joey too
Next comes wombat looking just like Will Young
'I think I better leave right now' is what he sung
Slithering on his belly Simon Cowell rushes to his seat
Ass ussual he just ssitss and never hissess to the beat
Here comes Dingo Darius, what is on his mind?
Remembering the words to 'Colour Blind'
The awards have been presented
The speeches have been read
The animals very silently
All creep off to bed.

Zoe Rogers (11)
Sir John Offley CE (VC) Primary School

France

F rench cheeses come in all shapes and sizes
R ich people like to drink wine
A rt is famous in France
N ancy is a place in France
C ities are wonderful
E uros are used in France.

Georgia Sorrentino (9)
Sir John Offley CE (VC) Primary School

France

F un and games are in Paris
R ivers are long in France
A rt is famous in France
N ice people live in France
C heese and wine is beautiful in France
E iffel Tower is over 300 metres high.

Elliott Francis (9)
Sir John Offley CE (VC) Primary School

Australia Animals

A boriginal art
U nique animals
S urfing through the sea
T erritory
R ainforest and mountains
A rt
L eaning outside
I talian, Vietnamese
A borgines have old dances

A wombat
N aughty dingo
I t was an amazing moment
M arvellous animals racing past
A red-back spider scurries at the side
L izards crawling
S piders sparkling.

Charlotte Austin (11)
Sir John Offley CE (VC) Primary School

The Amusing Aussie Animals

The coyote is trying to conduct the crowd while
A wallaby and a wombat are whistling loud,
The scorpions are banging their tails on the ground,
In tune with the banjos loud!

A platypus playing the piano,
A joey jiving jumpily,
A dingo dancing with a dolphin,
While a shark is doing a grinning smile.

The flamingo playing the flute,
A bandicoot belly-dancing while a crocodile is romancing,
While the ant is doing some Aboriginal art,
The closing ceremony is blown apart.

Megan Day (10)
Sir John Offley CE (VC) Primary School

Australia

A lligators are very snappy,
U p in the trees the monkeys swing from vine to vine,
S piders crawl all over you,
T asmanian devils are very vicious,
R attlesnakes are very dangerous,
A nimals are all over the jungle,
L eeches will suck all the blood out of your body,
I n the sea the sharks bite,
A nts sting everywhere on your bitten body,
N evertheless animals are lovely.

A ntelopes fight with their horns,
N othing makes a sound at night,
I n a tree the monkeys swing,
M onkeys are small and sneaky,
A nimals are all over the place,
L eopards sprint and pounce,
S corpions bite all the time.

Elliott Pointon (11)
Sir John Offley CE (VC) Primary School

The Thing

The thing awaits patiently,
It awaits patiently without a sound
Without a sound it scatters along with caution
It approaches with great caution
It's found the appropriate time
It comes, it's close, it's in no danger, it thinks.

The thing's bloodthirsty fangs dripping with beautiful taste
Whack! The beautiful taste will have to wait
As it needs to make its escape
Its escape needs to be great
Because it is the bait.

Andy Ridgway (10)
Sir John Offley CE (VC) Primary School

Strangest Things . . .

Today I went to Australia
And I saw the strangest thing . . .
A dingo playing the didgeridoo,
A kangaroo kicking a koala
And a bandicoot playing the bongos,
But unfortunately the numbat was nocturnal
And the frilled lizard was going frantic on the flute!
Then the possum started to play poker,
The roadrunner started to rock the rock climbing wall
And the wombat was just waking up,
The wallaby went over and walloped him,
The porcupine played the piano,
Then the weirdest thing happened,
I saw . . .
A potoroo paragliding!
That was my adventure in Australia,
Mum and Dad think I'm going mad.

Chloe Broad (10)
Sir John Offley CE (VC) Primary School

The Aussie Opera

K angaroos kissing a koala,
A wallaby whistling a tune,
N aughty turtles doing the tango, under the full moon,
G reedy crocodiles crunching a sheep,
A nd young joeys driving a jeep,
R aving rabbits racing a rodent,
O rang-utans aggravate the otters,
O livia octopus finds train spotters,
'S h!' she shouts.

Silence rules the bush once more.

Sarah Burton (11)
Sir John Offley CE (VC) Primary School

Australian Animals

A nimals are everywhere,
U p trees monkeys swing,
S corpions scatter along,
T asmanian devils beware,
R ats scatter on the ground,
A nimals are everywhere,
L ittle lions play all day,
I n the jungle lions roar,
A nimals are brilliant,
N aughty bears run at night.

A nimals are everywhere,
N othing makes a sound at night,
I n the jungle every animal sleeps,
M onkeys pinch your food,
A nimals are everywhere,
L izards sprint across the sandy roads,
S nakes slither across the floor.

Alexander Hedley (11)
Sir John Offley CE (VC) Primary School

Koala Bear

Koala bears
All cute and grey
Snuggling up
With their young on their back
But when darkness falls
They crawl down the eucalyptus tree
To search for leaves
Which should make a scrumptious snack
But when morning breaks
They crawl up the tree again
And then they rest.

Fiona Courthold (10)
Sir John Offley CE (VC) Primary School

I Saw . . .

I saw the kangaroo leaping
through the deep open fields.

I saw the koala's joey jump up
onto her mother's back.

I saw the Aborigines playing
the amazing didgeridoos.

I saw the dingo lie on the
glorious mountain tops.

I saw the platypus swim
through the ocean blue.

I saw the lizard climb the
rocks so hot.

I saw the turtle step and
take a break.

I saw . . .
all these things.

Yve Phillips (10)
Sir John Offley CE (VC) Primary School

Australia

A ustralia land all flat and dry,
U nique wildlife all colours and sizes,
S un and sea all hot and bothered,
T housands of people from all kinds of backgrounds,
R ivers and seas all blue and clear,
A boriginal languages which are unfamiliar,
L izards and koalas all fierce and fiery,
I talian and Greek live in Australia,
A boriginals sometimes have a bone through their noses.

Hannah Smith (11)
Sir John Offley CE (VC) Primary School

Australian Animals

A lways sunny even in winter
U nbelievable beaches miles long
S afaris of Australia must be cool
T asmanians can attack their prey
R apids rush all down the river
A mazing dingoes charge through the forest
L ightning strikes then the forest fire starts
I n the houses spiders crawl
A ll in the treetops monkeys swing
N asty bee stings hurt your arms

A lligators lurking in the lake
N aughty dingoes watch your every move
I nsects jump around on your back
M ountain tree frogs crawl on a branch
A nts fidgeting in the grass
L ittle creepy-crawlies tickle your feet
S nakes slither all through the night.

Ryan Heath (11)
Sir John Offley CE (VC) Primary School

Around The World I Go

The platypuses swimming like some eels,
The mother talking to her colony of seals,
The birds singing in trees so green,
The elder sitting like a victorious queen,
The koalas climbing for hours on end,
The animals are always your friend,
The kangaroos jumping, one, two, three,
They look so joyful playing happily,
The dingoes barking in the night,
If they wake you up, they will give you a fright.

Emma Dracup (10)
Sir John Offley CE (VC) Primary School

Australian Animals

A lligators snap all day long
U nlikely the chimps didn't nick my food
S corpion sitting scarcely stinging snakes
T asmanian devils ferocious again
R attlesnakes wriggle
A ny animals would charge but not the ostrich
L eeches suck your blood out of your body
I n the Australian bush the animals are awake
A nimals scatter quickly
N othing makes a sound at night

A ntelopes fight all day long
N othing runs as fast as the cheetah
I n the ocean the sharks tear their prey
M onkeys fool around
A nts march as long as the day goes by
L eopards pounce as hard as a punch
S nakes bite throughout the bush.

Dean Crutchley (11)
Sir John Offley CE (VC) Primary School

Africa

A is for Africa that burns hot in the sun
F is for fish swimming past my feet and splashing me
R is for rhinos that have big horns and poke me in my back
I is for insects that crawl up my neck and bite me
C is for cheetah which runs after me in the long grass
A is for antelope that jumps over me and cools me down.

Samantha Parkes (7)
Sir John Offley CE (VC) Primary School

Africa

A frica is a big country and the country stays hot
F rogs live in rainforests and some are poisonous
R ivers flow softly through Africa and into a sea or ocean
I ndian ocean lies off the coast of Africa
C heetahs chase their prey to eat
A nts are pests that crawl up your back and bite.

Daniel Brown (7)
Sir John Offley CE (VC) Primary School

Africa

A is for antelopes leaping in the plains
F is for flamingos by the riverside
R is for rainforest all dark and wet
I is for insects all creepy and scary
C is for cheetahs the fastest runner of them all
A is for the ants crawling past.

Evan Jones (8)
Sir John Offley CE (VC) Primary School

Africa

A is for antelope leaping over the plains
F is for flamingos, their feathers blowing in the warm breeze
R is for rivers trickling along the plain
I is for the Indian Ocean lapping the shores of Africa
C is for cheetahs catching their prey
A is for Africa with the burning sun on it.

Katey Valentine (7)
Sir John Offley CE (VC) Primary School

Africa

A is for Africa which is burning hot
F is for fish that swim in the African oceans
R is for rivers that people get water from
I is for the Indian Ocean that comes to an end by the beach
C is for the big cats which are very fierce
A is for alligator gliding through the water.

Elizabeth Courthold (8)
Sir John Offley CE (VC) Primary School

Africa

A is for Africa where the sun beats down
F is for fish that swim and splash me
R is for rhinos that run very fast
I is for the Indian Ocean that's lapping the shores
C is for crocodiles that have white teeth
A is for apples that are juicy and red.

Eleni Caulcott (7)
Sir John Offley CE (VC) Primary School

The Parthenon

The Parthenon is a historical building
that sits on top of the Acropolis.
It is still standing after the wars.
It was owned by Athena the goddess of wisdom.
While the Greeks rode past on a horse.
It was built in columns of marble and stone.
They carved and painted it with beautiful
colours and sculptures.
They built a huge statue of Athena
that stood inside it.

James Evans (9)
Whitby Heath Primary School

My Wings Take Me Home

Soaring through the skies, the king of all birds, I am a
majestic noble, fearless creature. My wings spread wide when
I fly. I am the golden eagle, king of America and the world.

I am a jungle bird, but I am also kept as a pet, my call
is recognisable throughout the jungle and my wings are more
colourful than the blossoming flower. I am a parrot the most exotic
of all birds.

During the cold, freezing winters, I sit on your garden fence,
chirping happily, bringing Christmas spirit to all, which is warmer
than any crackling fire. I am a robin, the merriest of all birds.

Gliding along lakes, my elegant head held high, I am a beauty
to the human eyes. I am a godsend and people have performed
ballets about me. I am a swan, a glorious, gliding beauty.

Alike the swan, I am a beauty to human eyes, with my
blue, green and white feathers, I am highly attractive.
I am a peacock, a great feathery pillow.

I am a bird of goodness, bringing peace wherever I go.
God sent me from Heaven, to stop war and help the righteous,
I also signify love. I am a dove, a love bird.

The tallest of them all and a fast runner, I am the biggest
bird since mammals appeared on land. My neck and head bald,
I don't need a haircut. I am an ostrich, a giant giant.

The sweetest of songs I sing, beak of gold and feathers coal-black.
I am the human friend all year round. I am so magical
it's as if a wizard has touched me. I am a blackbird, the magic bird.

Over the sea's weather fine, wind or bad, I never get sick
and the sun always touches my back. I often remind good humans
of happy memories and seaside days. I am a seagull, a calling
reminder of bright days.

So, with all these wings beating, I am the author of this poem, the
wise and intelligent owl and I too am a bird with wings known as
a bird of knowledge. But for now, my wings will take me home.

Rebecca McHugh (11)
Whitby Heath Primary School

Schooldays

The weekend is over and it's a sunny day,
My favourite day of the week has to be Monday,
After maths I can't wait to go out and play
And hope to see my two best friends Amy and May.

Soon it's going to be winter
And I don't think we're going to have much play,
When it rains and rains, it's going to be wet all day.

Today is Tuesday, sunny and bright,
I can't wait till school is over,
Because I go dancing tonight.

Wednesday and Thursday have gone so quick
And we've done some auditions for Oliver Twist and
I wonder who'll they'll pick?

The school week has gone and I had fun
And it seems like it's only just begun.

Abigail Rigby (9)
Whitby Heath Primary School

What I Want To Be

When I get older I want to be an astronaut and fly away into space.
When I get older I want to be an actress and be on TV, on
Home and Away.
When I get older I want to be a football player and score goals
for the team.
When I get older I want to be a dancer and star in my own show.
When I get older I want to be a police officer and send bad
people to jail.
When I get older I want to be a doctor and make ill people better.
When I get older I want to be . . .
Everything!

Danielle Aspinall (11)
Whitby Heath Primary School

What Is Blue?

Blue is the sea
crashing on the shore

Blue is the sky
up high.

Blue is the colour
of my bedroom floor.

Blue is the bluebells
growing in the wood.

Blue is the colour
of the tumbling waterfall.

Blue is the colour of
my dad's sparkling eyes.

Blue is the colour of my wet
swimming bag.

Blue is the best colour
of them all.

Shaun McGonagle (8)
Whitby Heath Primary School

Snow Poem

Crispy and just
Like snowflakes
In the winter when
I go out in the snow
I make snowballs
With my mum and dad
And brother
When I go to bed
I think about
Snow every night!

Lauren Carr (8)
Whitby Heath Primary School

Rainbow

Red is for hot fire
Blue is for the sky above
Yellow is for a sunny day
Green is for a dream today
Orange is for a melting ice pop on a stick
Pink is for the gleaming sunset
Purple is for a juicy grape
But most of all I like the rainbow.

Laura Fletcher (8)
Whitby Heath Primary School

The Horse

The horse is black and white,
Roger is his name,
His eyes are big and friendly
And he has a silky mane,
He likes to eat a carrot,
Apples, oats and hay,
But most of all he likes a good brush
Each and every day!

Melissa Williams (8)
Whitby Heath Primary School

What Is Blue?

Blue is the sea waving about,
Blue is for Everton, the best about,
Blue is the sky high above,
Blue is part of the globe,
Blue is very cold about,
Blue is the swimming pool, cool and clear,
Blue is a really good colour.

Jessica Chambers (8)
Whitby Heath Primary School

Food I Like

It seems the food I like to eat
Is just no good for me,
It also fills me up of course,
So I don't eat my tea.

My mum says I can have a snack,
As long as it is green,
Kiwi, apples, pears or grapes,
I think she's really mean.

For dinner at school I usually have
Sausages, beans and mash,
I'd eat a lot of other things too
If only I had the cash.

I'd much prefer a bag of crisps,
A chocolate bar or two,
But my dad says, 'You can't have that
Because it's not good for you.'

When my mum says, 'What do you want for tea?'
I ask for fish and chips,
But Mum says, 'No, I'll want some too
But I'll put weight on around my hips.'

My mum and dad are so unkind,
I have to eat just what they say,
But when I grow up and I leave home,
I'll have chocolate *every day!*

Lori Bartley (11)
Whitby Heath Primary School

Holiday

We've packed our cases
We're ready to fly
To a foreign place
Where the temperature is high.

Harry Davies-Jenkins (7)
Whitby Heath Primary School

Animal Fun

A is for an ant running everywhere,
B is for a badger covered in fuzzy hair,
C is for chameleon with its camouflaged skin,
D is for dog which scrounges in your bin,
E is for an elephant with its long grey trunk,
F is for a frog that loves to jump,
G is for a giraffe with its long neck,
H is for a horse proud with its rosette,
I is for iguana that lies in the sun,
J is for jaguar that likes to jump and run,
K is for a koala that lives in the trees,
L is for a lion that lies in the breeze,
M is for a mouse no lighter than a match,
N is for a nit that makes us all scratch,
O is for an ostrich the biggest bird on land,
P is for a pelican that lives by the sand,
Q is for the queen bee bossing bees around,
R is for a rabbit that doesn't make a sound,
S is for a sheep with a woolly back,
T is for a tiger with orange stripes and black,
U is for unicorn with its long, pointy horn,
V is for a vixen with its new baby born,
W is for a wolf howling in the night,
X is for a oxen exploring all in sight,
Y is for a yak with its big, long nose,
Z is for a zebra that everybody knows!

Helen Lyth (8)
Whitby Heath Primary School

Snowflakes

When it's snowing snowflakes come
They are all sorts of sizes
They are any colour too
And sometimes they melt on your tongue
And I love them.

Olivia Harvey (8)
Whitby Heath Primary School

Dreams

You spend your best time dreaming
It happens when you close your eyes
Sometimes you dream when you're awake
That's the big surprise

Daydreaming in the daytime
You plan your future days
A scientist, a doctor
Or an actor in top plays.

Ashleigh Fletcher (10)
Whitby Heath Primary School

Snow

In the night
I saw something
It was ice
I saw it twice
It was snow
It glowed so bright
Nearly all the town was covered in white.

Tammie Binks (9)
Whitby Heath Primary School

Snow Poem

Snowflakes are so white
They fall softly from the sky
We can make a snowflake
They are so much fun
Snow softly when we're all asleep
Snow is the best
You can make snowmen and snowballs
And throw them at anyone you like.

Faye Barrett (8)
Whitby Heath Primary School

A Holiday Is . . .

A holiday is full of fun
A holiday is to rest my brain
A holiday is a day out
A holiday is to sunbathe on the beach
A holiday is to eat ice cream every day
A holiday is to *splash!* in water
A holiday is to make a sandcastle
A holiday is to have a fight with my sis
A holiday is to go to a pool
A holiday is just to have *fun!*

Hannah Weston (9)
Whitby Heath Primary School

Snow, Snow

Snow, snow is so nice,
Snow, snow is quieter than mice,
Throwing snowballs,
Snow, snow is so bright,
The snow falls,
Snow is tight and also light,
I love snow,
Every night I see a glow of beautiful snow.

Alisha Paige Heppell (9)
Whitby Heath Primary School

Snow Poem

When everyone was in bed on a cold night,
I woke up to see the most amazing sight,
I drew back the curtains and saw all over
The lawn were piles of snow,
I ran to the door, ran out on the lawn,
Oh I love it when it snows.

Zoë Ambrose (8)
Whitby Heath Primary School

Pancake

Toss a pancake
Throw a pancake
At your mum

Toss a pancake
Throw a pancake
At your dad's bum

Toss a pancake
Throw a pancake
Filled with rum

Pancake, pancake
Stay in my tum.

Oliver Wedgwood (8)
Whitby Heath Primary School

Fat Fairy

There was a fat fairy
She flew very high
There was a fat fairy
She flew up to the sky
There was a fat fairy
Who lived in the dairy
There was a fat fairy
Who was very scary
And she was called Mary.

Rebecca Donnelly (8)
Whitby Heath Primary School

The Tooth Fairy

I am just a little fairy
Who flies around all day
To look for someone special
Who had been good all day
But when I find them I say
'Have you ever had a tooth
Bigger than my toe?'
And ask them to say yes or no
And if you say yes then you are my guest
To be like all the rest
To be able to fly all day.

Sophie Campbell (8)
Whitby Heath Primary School

Pony, Pony

Pony, pony, tail is bright,
Mane is soft to reflect the light.

Pony, pony, you'll just want to ride him,
Really soft to attract the children.

I ride so fast on my valiant steed,
Stop for a minute, then take the lead.

Pony, pony, you are so fine,
Pony, pony, I wish you were mine.

Eve Pemberton (8)
Whitby Heath Primary School

A Summer Holiday!

A summer holiday is fun, (sometimes)
A summer holiday is to eat ice cream,
A summer holiday is to snorkel in the sea,
A summer holiday is to relax by the pool,
A summer holiday is going to eat at a fancy café,
A summer holiday is to drink alcohol,
A summer holiday is to dance all night,
A summer holiday is to have a long lie in,
A summer holiday is to bomb into the pool,
A summer holiday is to cover yourself in make-up,
A summer holiday is to play beach ball,
A summer holiday is to build sandcastles,
A summer holiday is to drink Bucks Fizz,
A summer holiday is to explore the jungle,
A summer holiday is to dump homework,
A summer holiday is to give your brain a rest,
A summer holiday is to have a barbecue,
A summer holiday is to mess about,
A summer holiday is to practise hairdos,
A summer holiday is to make sand boats,
A summer holiday is to swallow the sea,
A summer holiday is to get a nice tan,
A summer holiday is to get red-hot sunburn,
A summer holiday is to read books,
A summer holiday is to go shopping,
A summer holiday is to wear your Burberry cap,
A summer holiday is to put on your best shoes,
A summer holiday is really the best thing ever,
A summer holiday is a summer holiday.

Zoe Seymour (10)
Whitby Heath Primary School

A Little Weather Poem

Sarah is cold and covered in snow
But there is a house where she can go

Suzie and Penny go walking together
They visit their friends in the windy weather

Every day it rains more and more
And the puddles get deeper than ever before

Hooray! Today is a sunny day
So snakes and ladders is the game to play.

Amy Hughes (9)
Whitby Heath Primary School

Snowflake

Snow falls from the sky,
Small snowflakes dropping by,
Makes a carpet on the ground,
Falling, falling with no sound,
Making snowmen is such fun,
Praying there will be no sun,
To melt the glistening glowing snow,
I love the snow clear and crunchy, glow, glow, glow.

Chloë Moore (8)
Whitby Heath Primary School

Snow

White is snow falling from the sky
Snow is cold on a winter day
Snow leaves everything white
Snow turns trees into snowmen
Snow is wonderful.

Daniel Sheldon (8)
Whitby Heath Primary School

The Ride

Walking through
The coloured gates
Eager to find my
Parents' fates

Striding right
Into the queue
Waiting, waiting
That's what to do

We see the first lot
So not slow
My dad bottles out
He (says he) has to go

The excitement
Is growing
The coaster
Is slowing

At last it is
Our turn
My stomach
Begins to churn

Finally I see reality
It's something that I want to miss
I suddenly realise
I don't want to go on this

I sit down
I grip the bar
I check the coaster
Oh how so far!

Off we go
Lightning speed
This is a fast ride
Yes, indeed

Down the slope
Round the bend
Will this ride
Ever end?

At last we're slowing down
Is this the end?
No, it's a slope
Haven't I even got one friend?

Going down
A winding track
Can't I, can't I
Go right back?

Oh dear
My true dread
The loop-the-loop
Blood rushing to the head

At last the ride
Has past
I'm not the first
And I'm not the last

The ride has
Driven me insane
But I ask my mum
'Can I go on it again?'

Samuel Clayton (10)
Wimboldsley Community Primary School

Horse Chestnut Tree

Monday - is the first day of the week
We see the tree before we work
As steady as a rock

Tuesday - is the second day of the week
We see the tree, we're going to work
Around the clock

Wednesday - is the third day of the week
We see the tree rustling
In the breeze

Thursday - is the fourth day of the week
We spy the tree, we stand and stare

Friday - is the fifth day of the week
We say goodbye to our friend, the tree.

Charlotte Barber (9)
Wimboldsley Community Primary School

Mountain Poem

So high that you could almost fasten the tops to the sky,
So vast that you could look but never see the peaks,
So coloured that you would take days to note down the first three,
So beautiful and majestic, so high and mighty
Is the mountain, that's right in front of me.

Helen Powell (10)
Woodfall Junior School

Death Of A Lion - Haiku

Lonely, sly python
Yellow slithering attack
On deadly lion.

Jake Johnson (10)
Woodfall Junior School

Happiness

Happiness is red like a poppy
It smells like the reddest rose
It feels like lovely fresh air swishing towards you
It tastes like melted chocolate
Happiness looks like the shining sun
It sounds like fruit
Jingling in the trees.

Laura Pope (9)
Woodfall Junior School

Joy

Joy is red like a rose
Joy smells like a daisy
Joy tastes like a breath of fresh air
Joy looks like a sweet baby
Joy sounds like happy children.

Jemma Louise Anyon (9)
Woodfall Junior School

Peace

Peace is blue like the morning sky
Peace tastes like strawberries
Peace smells like perfume
Peace looks like a rainbow
Peace sounds like bells
Peace feels like silk.

Megan Hall (9)
Woodfall Junior School

Fairy Tale

F airy godmothers will grant your wishes
A wicked witch will curse you
I like Prince Charming
R eally, really ugly sisters
Y ellow, golden, sparkly dress

T hree little pigs and the big bad wolf
A laddin and the genie
L ovely golden, sparkly dress
E nchanted with a spell.

Wesley Osunjimi (8)
Woodfall Junior School

Happiness

Happiness is blue like the bright blue morning sky,
It tastes like warm melting toffee apples,
It smells like a beautiful red rose,
It looks like a beautiful bird flying gently through the sky,
It sounds like the laughter of children having fun.

Catherine Halton (9)
Woodfall Junior School

Hate

The colour is black,
It tastes like cabbage,
Hate smells like rubbish,
Hate looks like monsters under the bed,
It sounds like thunderbolts,
Hate feels like dragons around you.

Callum Reid (8)
Woodfall Junior School

Cinderella

C inderella married the prince,
I n a romantic church,
N orman was the prince's name,
D en was the best man,
E veryone was happy,
R ed cherries were on the cake,
E veryone danced
L ovely red roses were thrown at them,
L ovely violets were thrown at them
A nd some confetti.

David Nevin-Jones (8)
Woodfall Junior School

Happiness

Happiness is orange like the sun's burning rays
It tastes like melting chocolate
Happiness smells like pink roses
It looks like robins flying across the big blue sky
Happiness sounds like children playing in the playground.

Rohan Littler (9)
Woodfall Junior School

Love

Love is like red roses that twinkle from the fluttering sky,
It tastes like sweet strawberries,
It smells like tulip flowers, like orange flavour,
Love looks like purple and pink swirls everywhere,
Love sounds like the cold breeze,
It feels like the warm air around you.

Sophie Smith (9)
Woodfall Junior School

Peter Pan

P eter Pan magic man,
E very night takes a flight.
T eeth so white, magic light.
E ven though he flies, he's always in disguise.
R un away to Never Never Land

P reparing to get Hook.
A ll aboard, onto the ship.
N ever Never Land is a magical place.

Jake Bayliff (8)
Woodfall Junior School

Sadness

Sadness is like the darkness of the night,
It tastes like horrible black jacks,
It smells like a dump,
It looks like blood,
It sounds like a dog howling in the night,
It feels like ghastly rough fur.

Georgina Peacock (9)
Woodfall Junior School

Happiness

Happiness is yellow
Like the burning sun
It tastes like icing on a cake
It smells like rice with spicy chicken.

Leigh Maxwell (9)
Woodfall Junior School

Rapunzel

R apunzel is beautiful, a prince would die for her.
A wicked witch captured the beautiful Rapunzel.
P oor Rapunzel trapped in the witch's chamber.
U p in the witch's palace she broke out of her chamber.
N ever stopped telling her unicorn to stop.
Z igzag sword is very spooky.
E legant Rapunzel is terrified.
L ate Rapunzel to get back home to the prince.

Jack Hughes (7)
Woodfall Junior School

Fear

Fear tastes like junk
Fear smells like rotten cheese
It looks like blood
Fear sounds like the screeching of the blackbird
It feels like gook.

Ryan Green (9)
Woodfall Junior School

Love

Love is red like the burning fire,
It tastes like a strawberry yoghurt,
Love smells like a sweet scent of strawberries,
It looks like a cute bright sweetheart,
Love sounds like a sweet scent from the wind,
It feels like a heart beating really fast.

Ellie Jones (8)
Woodfall Junior School

Fairy Tales

F airy tales are really good to read
A t the dwarfs' house Snow White is scared
I ncredible dress for Cinderella
R apunzel has long hair
Y esterday Cinderella got married

T omorrow is the prince's ball
A t twelve, Cinderella is sad
L ots of men like Beauty
E lves are tiny
S now White is beautiful.

Jack Mellor (8)
Woodfall Junior School

Love

Love is red and pink like blossom falling from the trees,
Love tastes like chocolates,
It smells like creamy marshmallows over a burning fire,
Love looks like a red heart twinkling up above in the light blue sky,
It sounds like a robin singing sweetly,
Love feels like a warm summer evening.

Esther Clarke (9)
Woodfall Junior School

Happiness

Happiness is yellow like a burning sun
It tastes like a piece of cake
It smells like a cooked dinner.

Jessica Hall (9)
Woodfall Junior School

Fairy Tale

F is for fairy tales which are fun to read
A is for adventures in all kinds of ways
I is for incredible in lots of fairy tale stories
R is for rags but Cinderella's rags turned into a beautiful dress
Y is for yellow which was the colour of Cinderella's dress

T is for tatty clothes that Cinderella had
A is for angels that come down to care
L is for lying, which the sisters did to the prince
E is for ending that's always happy.

Joshua Cooke (7)
Woodfall Junior School

Happiness

Happiness as bright as a melon
It tastes like blue and green jelly sweets
It smells like summer fruits
It looks like the waves on the sea
It sounds like a mermaid singing
It feels like my snugly bed.

Chloe Metcalf-White (8)
Woodfall Junior School

Love

Love is red like a lovely red rose,
Love tastes like strawberry flavoured ice cream,
It smells like scented perfume,
Love sounds like baby birds tweeting in the morning,
It feels like a lovely warm fire.

Georgia-mai Timms (8)
Woodfall Junior School

Snow White

S now falls when Snow White passes,
N o one has seen Snow White before,
O n a summer's day Snow White ate a poisoned apple,
W hen Snow White found a prince she and the prince got married,

W hen Snow White saw the prince and she had married him
    they were happy
H e was very, very rich and they went home on a horse they bought
I n the house were seven little beds
T hey were so happy to see Snow White home so early
E veryone was happy so they decided to have a party.

Amy Jones (7)
Woodfall Junior School

Happiness

Happiness is red like a roaring fire,
It tastes like hot curry sauce,
It smells like a roasted turkey,
It looks like a deep red rose,
It sounds like the whistling wind,
It feels like a soft blanket.

Sean Lindley (8)
Woodfall Junior School

Happiness

Happiness is blue, it's like the sky,
It tastes like the sparkly water,
It smells like the shiny clouds,
It looks like the smiley face,
It sounds like the windy sky,
It feels like love.

John Collins (9)
Woodfall Junior School

Fairy Tales

F airy tales are fun to read and really good
A laddin has a flying carpet, I would like one
I nside the palace Cinderella and the prince dance
R apunzel has very long hair
Y ou look like Snow White

T emptation takes Cinderella to the ball
A wonderful castle upon a hill
L ove is all around us
E nchanted palaces everywhere
S uch happy endings to every tale.

Rachel Knox (8)
Woodfall Junior School

Fear

Fear is black like twelve o'clock at night
Fear tastes like a horrible bug
Fear smells like cooking an omelette
Fear looks like a squished bug
Fear sounds like a witch's cackle
Fear feels like a squirming worm.

Jacob Shepherd (8)
Woodfall Junior School

Happiness

Happiness is kind
Bright coloured and shiny
It tastes like mint
It smells like chocolate
It looks like Sweetie Land
It sounds like buzzing bees and tweeting birds
It feels like the sunset.

Alex Webb (9)
Woodfall Junior School

The Shoemaker

T he shoemaker was poor
H e had no money
E lves came to help at night

S hoes they made of leather
H ow beautiful they were
O ne day he sold the shoes
E lves helped him for many days
M aking him more shoes
A nd they made him very rich
K ind elves making shoes
E very elf helped
R oyalty came to buy the shoes.

William Millington (7)
Woodfall Junior School

Aladdin

A laddin was a poor young boy who lived on the streets
L amp shining gold
A laddin found the lamp in the cave
D reaming of being rich
D ancing with Princess Jasmin
I mpressive jewels in the cave
N asty, evil emperor.

Jordan Stuart (7)
Woodfall Junior School

Cinderella

C inderella got trapped in the attic to do all the work
I nside the attic it was dark and full of nasty rats
   that nibbled her feet
N asty sisters make her do all the housework
'D o all the housework,' that's all her sisters say
E xactly midnight everything changed back
R ats keep nibbling poor Cinderella's feet
E vil sisters make her do all the work
L onely Cinderella trapped in the attic
L ovely golden dress she wore at the ball
A ny old man would not dance with Cinderella.

Sarah Maxwell (7)
Woodfall Junior School

Snow White

S now glows gloriously on her pure, white, soft face
N o one hated Snow White except her evil stepmother
O ne day a witch came to the house and gave Snow White
   a rosy red apple
W ithin the witch was a heart of blackness

W ishing, that's what the dwarfs did for Snow White to live
H ow did Snow White awaken?
   The prince gave her his love with a kiss.
I n the prince's heart he loved her with all his heart
T rembling, the prince cried and cried and she woke
E ventually they got back to the glorious palace.

Beth Lawley (8)
Woodfall Junior School